BILLY FINN

The Greatest Basketball Player I Ever Saw

PREFACE

Hello Len,

Thank you for the book "Billy Finn"! I love your passion for basketball and enjoyed reading your book. Since you witnessed USC/UCLA games with Bob Boyd, John Wooden, & Lew Alcindor, you certainly have seen some of the best Trojans & Bruins of all-time.

All the best to you (and your book sales!).

Andy Enfield

UNIVERSITY OF SOUTHERN CALIFORNIA • GALEN CENTER
3400 SOUTH FIGUEROA STREET • LOS ANGELES, CA 90089-2360
TELEPHONE: (213) 740-3815 • FAX: (213) 740-7586 • WWW.USCTROJANS.COM

Declaration of Dr. Len Bergantino

I, DR. LEN BERGANTINO, DECLARE:

The picture of Billy Finn used in this book was given to me in 1961 by Billy Finn, himself.

The foregoing is true and correct and I would and could testify as such in a court of law if called upon to do so.

This declaration was written in Los Angeles, California on March 5, 2020.

____
DR. LEN BERGANTINO

BILLY FINN

The Greatest Basketball Player I Ever Saw

Len Bergantino

InfusedMedia Co. LLC
www.infusedmedia.co
1-888-251-6088

ACKNOWLEDGEMENT

XLIBRIS PUBLISHING COMPANY PERSONNEL:

MICHELLE POSTRANO IS A MANAGER WHO GETS THINGS UNSTUCK IN THE MYRIAD OF PLACES THEY CAN GET STUCK AND GETS PROJECTS COMPLETED. BION, THE GREAT BRITISH PSYCHOANALYST SAID "THERE ARE TWO NASTY FACTS. THE FIRST IS THAT PEOPLE NEED TO DEPEND ON OTHER PEOPLE AND THE SECOND IS THAT YOU HAVE TO FIND SOMEONE WHO IS DEPENDWORTHY." MICHELLE POSTRANO IS DEPENDWORTHY.

MONIQUE GOMEZ IS GIFTED. SHE HAS THE ABILITY TO SPEAK TO SOMEONE AND HELP THEM RECOGNIZE THEIR DEEPEST WISH AND THEN PUT THAT WISH INTO PUBLISHING ACTION.

FOR ME PUBLISHING A BOOK IS A NIGHTMARE. MY FIRST BOOK BECAME A MASTER CLASSIC IN THE FIELD IN 1981 -"Psychotherapy, Insight & Style: The Existential Moment, published by Allyn & Bacon, Inc., Boston, 288 pp.) The experience was so torturous that I did not do another book until November 18, 2018. I have done 9 more since then. Xlibris personnel that were helpful in their various company duties and assignments were:

Richard Tecson, Cindy Murray, Carlos Cortes and Joy Daniels.

And of course there was Billy Finn, the greatest basketball player whoever lived, who trained me to become and know enough about basketball to have written this book and to cousin Fred Bredice who could shoot at a level where he hardly ever hit the rim, and only net!

As for the Black Brothers there were many along the way in the fields of sports, music (Miles Davis), education (Lou Thomas), Shirley Jones (co-founder of the Kedren Community Mental Health Center in South

Central Los Angeles, and PSYCHIATRIST PAUL LOGAN, M.D. WHO GAVE ME A CHANCE WHEN NO ONE ELSE WOULD BECAUSE HE STATED "I UNDERSTAND BLACK RAGE!"

THE REVEREND DR. LEN BERGANTINO

CONTENTS

Introduction to the Greatest Basketball Player I Ever Saw

First I must spell out my view of "greatness" and give a few specific examples in the area of basketball so the reader will have a way to correctly assess the basketball knowledge, wisdom and savvy of the author.

While this may sound like an inauspicious and less than humble way to begin my treatise, THIS IS NOT A BOOK ABOUT HUMILITY BUT ABOUT ONE OF A KIND EXCELLENCE EVALUATED BY SOMEONE WITH THE BASKETBALL CHOPS TO MAKE SUCH AN ASSESSMENT.

I define greatness as an ability or skill in one's chosen endeavor that society as a whole is perhaps likely to experience once in a lifetime or perhaps a few times. I spent 44 years studying, coaching and playing basketball at differing levels of involvement and I have paranormal abilities, which means at best you will have no way to correctly evaluate me, the evaluator.

At the professional level the first time I gave a thought to greatness was in 1957 when I saw Elgin Baylor playing for Seattle University throw a turn around jump shot while hanging in the air on the left side of the court past the foul line and not quite as far out as the key. Basically Baylor revolutionized basketball in that from that shot every kid in America was trying to imitate him and the game was never the same again in that Baylor added a level of movement to an otherwise still game.

I was a shooter and interested in pure shooters. Bill Sharman, the USC All-American of 1948 was such a shooter. My cousin, Little All American

Fred Bredice told me he saw Sharman make 100 fouls in a row out of 100 attempts at Bob Cousy's Camp at Camp graylag in New Hampshire. Larry Bird was a pure shooter. I saw him make 18 in a row from past the circle on the left side of the court at the Forum in 1977 (Lakers-Celtics).

While Babe Ruth would certainly be in this conversation, the most dominant athlete I ever saw was Bill Russell, the 6 ft. 9 in. center of the Boston Celtics. The Celtics never won a championship before he got there and they won eleven out of thirteen world championships when he was there. I remember his reflexes as a defender were unbelievable Furthur, he was the inventor of the famous Boston Celtic fast break in that immediately upon snaring a rebound he would throw at least a half court pass to the side and the Celtics were off and running!

I met Bill Russell on two occasions. The first was at a Providence College basketball game around 1960. His brother-in-law Jim Hadnot was playing Center for Providence College. I believe Joe Mullaney was the coach, later to become coach of the Los Angeles Lakers. My friend, Johnny Mango, stopped him and said, "Bill, what do you think of Jim Hadnot?" Russell looked up for about 30 seconds and then said, "Big Jim has been a tremendous disappointment to the family.

Red Auerbach was Russell's coach, and no one had seen the likes of Bill Russell when he came to the Celtics, SO AUERBACH SAID, "GIVE RUSSELL THE BALL AND GET THE HELL OUT OF HIS WAY AND LET HIM CREATE WHATEVER KIND OF GAME HE ENVISIONS!" This was stated in a book called "RED AND ME" BY BILL RUSSELL! Prior to reading that book I brought my developmentally delayed son to the Sports Club LA where Russell was a guest helping out an MD who specialized in pain control. I asked Russell if he would take a picture with my son. I later heard he never took pictures with anybody and White guys messed him over pretty badly when the Celtics traveled South, so much so that Red Auerbach told a motel or hotel owner that unless he accomodated Russell along with the rest of the team, the Celtics would never stay there again!

Russell took one look at my developmentally delayed son and in a split second the gears of his mind did an about face, realizing this had nothing to do with black or White and he took the picture! Russell is one of the brightest athletes I ever met and if I were to guess having been a clinical psychologist for 42 years, I would say his IQ is over 140!

AS FOR RED AUERBACH, IT TOOK A GREAT COACH NOT

TO COACH! MOST COACHES WOULD HAVE BEEN STUPID BASTARDS THAT TRIED TO FIT RUSSELL INTO THEIR SYSTEM SO THEY COULD AT LEAST GIVE THE APPEARANCE OF COACHING EVEN THOUGH THEIR TEAMS WOULD BE LUCKY TO BREAK OVER .500! I wish I could personally beat the living shit out of any and all coaches who destroyed players lives and careers by not being able to utilize an individual player's God Given Talents while forcing them into a system that is pedantically death producing as opposed to evoking a one of a kind experience filled with the excitement that only the rare greatness of an athlete can generate! Auerbach on the other hand said, "Give Russell the ball, and get the fuck out of his way!"

THE RESULT ELEVEN OUT OF THIRTEEN YEARS BILL RUSSELL AND THE BOSTON CELTICS WERE WORLD CHAMPIONS!

<u>GREAT SHOOTERS DON'T HIT THE RIM</u>

The first time I saw Stephen Curry play for Davidson College I knew he was a great shooter! His shots were pure net. He never hit the rim!

Things I did to become a pure shooter were:

1. Play basketball on the outdoor courts when it was night time. If you get pure net when it is dark outside you will get pure net in the daylight.

2. In the kitchen of the house in which I grew up there were little knobs to open and close the cabinets where dishes were stored. With a damp kitchen towel I used to make 7 out of 10 times the dishtowel hang on the hook throwing jump shots or hook shots from anywhere in the kitchen. I used to love to play one on one with my friends and whip their asses with this dampened towel for money!

3. On days in which there was no school I would roll a piece of toilet paper into a little ball, stand 15 feet away just outside the bathroom door, and throw eight of ten on average spitballs through a 1 1/2 inch deep 3-4 inch wide soap dish that was part and parcel of the bathtub! After that, shooting on a basketball court was easy.

JERRY WEST WAS A GREAT CLUTCH SHOOTER
BUT I HATED WATCHING HIM SHOOT! HE
USED TO BANG THE BASKETBALL OFF THE
RIM ON THE WAY IN! THUS, I SAY HE WAS A
GREAT CLUTCH SHOOTER WHO WON A LOT
OF GAMES AT THE BUZZER, BUT HE WAS NOT
A GREAT SHOOTER!

A GREAT COLLEGE SHOOTER -MID FIFTIES -JACK THE
SHOT FOLEY WHO AVERAGED 41 POINTS A GAME FOR HOLY
CROSS IN WORCESTER, MA
GREAT BALL HANDLERS

1. Bob Cousy - All American from Holy Cross in 1954 Cousy had
   peripheral vision and used to dribble, pass behind his back, and
   hit open players others did not see because they did not have
   peripheral vision. In other words Cousy could see all the way
   around his body including the back of his head. Furthur, he
   would put on dribbling exhibitions before the 24 second rule came
   into professional basketball. He would often put on a dribbling
   exhibition as the clock was winding down to end the game and
   then throw the ball as high as he could up into the air until the
   game ending buzzer sounded. While his shootins was a little better
   than average, as he threw a one hander while raising his right leg,
   he often missed the clutch shots that would win a game.
2. Marques Haynes used to put on dribbling exhibitions where he
   was all over the floor with the ball no farther than an inch and one
   half from the floor while a defensive player from the Washington
   Nationals chased this Harlem Globetrotter all over the Waterbury,
   Connecticut Armory.

I WAS INTERESTED IN PURSUING GREATNESS! I DIDN'T
PARTICULARLY CARE WHERE IT CAME FROM!!! NBA,
HARLEM GLOBETROTTERS, COLLEGE, HIGH SCHOOL,
ET. AL.
KOBE BRYANT - HAD THE GREATEST KILLER INSTINCT
I HAVE EVER SEEN IN ANY ATHLETE! He wasn't that big. He got

81 points in his prime and 64 points his last game, matching Elgin Baylor's 64 point game during his prime!

LEBRON JAMES HAS THE GREATEST UNDEFINABLE QUALITY OF GREATNESS I HAVE EVER SEEN IN ANY PROFESSIONAL ATHLETE.

If I looked at individual skills, there was always someone I thought had a greater individual skill. than Lebron James. However, he gave one the feeling when he drove down the lane to the basket and you were defending him THAT A QUARTER HORSE WAS COMING AT YOU!

LEBRON HAS BEEN ABLE TO GET WHATEVER TEAM HE PLAYS FOR TO OVERACHIEVE WINNING MULTIPLE CHAMPIONSHIPS IN THE MODERN DAY ERA! HE HAS THE ABILITY TO PUT FORTH SUPERHUMAN EFFORT ON A CONSISTENT BASIS EVEN WHEN OPPONENTS OUTMAN AND OUTGUN HIS TEAM! THE DEGREE TO WHICH HE IS ABLE TO DO THIS I HAVE NEVER SEEN BEFORE IN MY LIFETIME AND I BELIEVE TO BE A ONE OF A KIND ABILITY THAT CAN BE DEFINED AS "GREATNESS"

This being said, I have not seen Michael Jordan on a consistent enough basis to have an evaluation. The only full game I saw him play was in the NCAA Championship for North Carolina when he was a junior and James Worthy was a senior.

SO WHICH ONE OF THESE PLAYERS IS THE GREATEST BASKETBALL PLAYER OF ALL TIME? WHICH ONE COULD HAVE BEEN IN A ROBERT REDFORD MOVIE ABOUT A BASKETBALL PLAYER INSTEAD OF A BASEBALL PLAYER CALLED "THE NATURAL". HOW ABOUT, NONE OF THE ABOVE!

THE BEST BASKETBALL PLAYER I EVER SAW WAS A KID NAMED BILLY FINN WHO HAD HALF HIS HEAD TAKEN OFF IN AN AUTOMOBILE ACCIDENT RIGHT AFTER HIGH SCHOOL!

I Knew Billy Finn
From 1957-1961

I was eighteen years old when I last saw him. Since then I received a B.A., M.A., M.S.Ed., an E.d.D. and Ph.D. and I have become an internationally renown psychologist, professional musician, public school teacher and counselor, and have coached basketball and been a referee of basketball in addition to coaching baseball and being an umpire AND I TELL YOU BILLY FINN WAS THE GREATEST BASKETBALL PLAYER WHOEVER LIVED!

As I write this book it is the last book I plan to write at the age of 76 years old; and it was on my bucket list of things to do before I die because I am one of a few remaining both who actually saw him play basketball and who has the attention to detail to describe the kind of phenomena that made Billy Finn The Greatest Basketball Player Whoever Lived!

There is a former basketball referedd named Bill Guisto who knew how good Billy Finn was so I recently asked him to write a chapter for this book. I do not at this time know if he is willing or if he can write the details however I have enclosed the letter I sent him on March 1, 2020. That letter will follow this page.

March 1, 2020

Bill Guisto,

I want you to write a chapter of a book I have just begun working on that establishes Billy Finn as the greatest basketball player that ever lived.

While I have given adequate reasons for stating this, with such a claim things have to be spelled out very clearly.

You are the only other person other than myself WHO GOT THE MAGNITUDE OF FINN'S GREATNESS.

You told me his only competitor was Pete Maravich so I had my daughter get him on U-Tube a few years ago. I thought Finn was better because he was shorter and therefore his dribble and fast jerky burst was closer to the ground and generated more total apeshit excitement among 2000 or so fans stamping their feet at the Armory! In other words who would you rather watch? For a pro I loved watching Elgin Baylor the best, other than that if it were not for the intensity of the playoffs I wouldn't watch it at all!

Double spaced on a typewriter is fine. I do not know how to use computers.

I will need a permission to use your material under your name as my publisher has a section called content evaluation whereby they do not do anything without prior permission.

I just did a baseball book entitled WHEN BASEBALL WAS KING THE NEW YORK YANKEES WERE KING OF BASEBALL. (FLYER ENCLOSED)

All the books I have done can be found on drlenbergantino.com

I was Billy Finn's best friend in high school. I knew he was better than anybody else but who would have thought your high school buddy would turn out to be the best you ever saw fifty years later!!! I used to set up games at Fulton Park. I had Freddie Bredice, my cousin from Torrington, one of the greatest pure shooters I have ever seen along with Finn, Spencer, et. al. Finn had just completed his freshman year. Cousin Fred said, "Where did you find that kid Finn? MARS!" Maybe Cousin Fred saw it back then!

Sincerely,
Len Bergantino

BILLY FINN

BETTER THAN JORDAN!.. BETTER THAN
LE BRON! BETTER THAN MAGIC!

WRITTEN BY
THE REVEREND DR. LEN BERGANTINO, ED.D., PH.D., D. DIV.

1. Billy Finn at 5 ft. 10 inches tall about 165 pounds used to drive all the way down the right sideline into the corner and hook clean through the net with a right handed hook shot. He could also do this banking the ball off the backboard while dribbling and driving into the far left corner!

2. Billy Finn could drive down the left sideline and with his left hand hook from the corner clean through or off the backboard.

3. Billy Finn could hook either right or left handed from straight out past the foul circle.

4. It didn't matter how big the opponent, Billy Finn had a quick jerk movement to one side and in a split second the was by the opponent and in for a left handed or right handed hook or layup as he could go both ways.

5. Billy Finn had stomach muscles that looked like the old washerwoman's washboard. He used to run laps for hours and he virtually never got tired.

6. At the time Billy Finn went to Sacred Heart High School you could not go straight from high school to the pros! Basketball has suffered greatly from this indiscretion in that THE GENERAL PUBLIC NEVER GOT TO SEE A MICHAELANGELO PAINT HIS PICTURE ON THE BASKETBALL COURT!

7. I JUDGE BILLY FINN ON HIS ABILITY TO GENERATE EXCITEMENT AND INTEREST AMONG BASKETBALL FANS IN THAT WHEN HE PLAYED I GOT TO SEE THINGS I NEVER SAW BEFORE AND I NEVER SAW AGAIN!

8. In my day I could shoot as well as Bill Sharman of the Celtics, ON THE COURT BUT NOT ON THE FOUL LINE, My cousin Fred Bredice, All State Torrington High School, saw Sharman make 100 out of 100 at Bob Cousy's camp. I USED TO HANG OUT IN THE FAR CORNER, BILLY FINN WOULD MOVE THER OTHER 9 PLAYERS TO THE OTHER SIDE OF THE COURT, AND WITH THE FLICK OF HIS WRIST WHICH WAS LIKE A 2 by 4 piece of thick wood the ball would come to me all alone in the corner and I had ten points in two minutes on 5 straight shots.

9. THE REASON BILLY FINN LOVED ME AND I BECAME HIS BEST FRIEND WAS BECAUSE I HAD THE WISDOM TO KNOW "HE WAS BILLY FINN AND I WASN'T!"

10. If you looked to your right when he had the ball HE APPEARED TO BE FLOATING ON AIR!

11. No one had ever done this since 1960 -float on air and hit me five straight wide open with no one around me and 9 guys on the other side of the court, THEN:

12. I WAS PLAYING IN A FIVE ON FIVE PICKUP GAME AT THE SPORTS CLUB LOS ANGELES AND THE GUY FLOATED AND HIT ME FIVE IN A ROW AND I HAD TEN POINTS BEFORE THE THREE POINT SHOT WENT IN. I WAS SHOCKED, AND ALTHOUGH I HAD NOTHING TO COMPLAIN ABOUT, I SHOUTED! "WHO THE FUCK ARE YOU! YOU DON'T BELONG HERE! WHAT'S YOUR NAME AND WHAT DO YOU DO FOR A LIVING?!?!?" HE MATTER OF FACTLY SAID, "MY NAME IS MIKE DONLEAVY AND I COACH THE LOS ANGELES LAKERS." There were a lot of things Billy Finn could do that Mike Donleavy could not do, but he could float on air when he ran and get 9 guys to one side OF THE FLOOR! (with me wide open)

13. I came to the awareness on February 1, 2020 that MIKE DONLEAVY IS THE REINCARNATED SOUL OF BILLY FINN. IF YOU READ MY OTHER WORKS YOU WILL KNOW THAT I HAVE A DIRECT CONNECTION TO GOD AND I HAVE BEEN THRUST INTO THE ARENA OF GETTING A TIP OF THE ICEBERG GLIMPSE OF REINCARNATION IN THAT I AM MADE PRIVY TO A FEW OF THE PLAYERS BY NAME.

WRITING A BOOK IS A PAIN IN THE ASS AND WHEN MAKING STATEMENTS SUCH AS I HAVE JUST MADE I NOT ONLY HAVE TO DEAL WITH PASSIVE AGGRESSIVE PUBLISHERS BUT FOR THE MOST PART AN UNGRATEFUL PUNITIVE AUDIENCE WHOSE PRIMARY GOALS IN LIFE ARE TO AVOID THE CHAOS AND ANXIETY OF NOT KNOWING AND TO CONTEND THAT

WHAT I AM HERE ON A KARMIC MISSION TO IMPART TO YOU DOES NOT EXIST!

14. A Mike Donleavy's son played for Duke and then the pros. He played the same kind of game Billy Finn taught me how to play as a shooter-an interesting coincidence.
15. I have noticed that God is most pleased when I get it the first time. When you don't is when you get kicked in the ass; however, in this case God has me feeling compelled to write about events from 1957-1961 to complete my karmic mission, so I don't have to come back and do it again!

52 Points State Record Set In February, 1961

Elgin Baylor got 64 points in the pros; Kobe Bryant got 81 and Wilt Chamberlin got 100 points in one game! WHY THE HELL WOULD I CLAIM BILLY FINN WAS A BETTER BASKETBALL PLAYER THAN THEM! Incidentally Billy Finn's scoring record was eclipsed by Calvin Murphy who got 60 points in one game and played for the Houston Rockets for a number of years.

<u>IT WASN'T THE FACT FINN GOT 52, IT WAS THE WAY HE GOT THEM THAT I HAVE NEVER SEEN BEFORE OR SINCE!</u> His dribbling of a basketball was closer to the ground than Bob Cousy and half way between Bob Cousy and Marques Haynes of The Harlem Globetrotters, who used to put on dribbling exhibitions against The Washington Nationals on tour. IN ADDITION FINN HAD A JERKY MOVE THAT WAS FASTER THAN A FLASH OF LIGHT, AND WITH A JERKY ONE STEP THE BEST OF DEFENDERS WENT BACK ON THEIR HEELS ONLY TO FALL ON THEIR ASS! YOU HAD TO SEE IT TO BELIEVE IT!

BACK TO THE FIFTY TWO POINT GAME AGAINST NAUGATUCK HIGH SCHOOL. THE BEST DEFENSIVE PLAYER ALWAYS GUARDED BILLY FINN! FINN WITH HIS JERKY DRIBBLE, THREW THE BALL UNEXPECTEDLY THROUGH THE OPPONENTS LEGS, RAN AROUND BEHIND HIM TO RETRIEVE THE BALL, AND WENT IN FOR A LAYUP WHERE TWO THOUSAND PEOPLE AT THE WATERBURY ARMORY WENT ABSOLUTELY APESHIT!

For All Time in the Basketball Hall of Fame!

While there is a Billy Finn award, only those who are over 65 ever got to see him play and others younger have no idea what he actually did, or what you actually did.

On a personal preference level I THINK THE GAME OF BASKETBALL WHEN YOU PLAYED WAS A FINESSE GAME AND IT WOULD ALSO BE IMPORTANT TO HAVE THE BODY MOVEMENTS OF ELGIN BAYLOR IN HIS LAST YEAR AT SEATTLE AND EARLY YEARS WITH THE MINNEAPOLIS LAKERS, AS WELL AS THE PURE SHOOTING OF YOUR CLOSE FRIEND AND COLLEAGUE BILL SHARMAN INCLUDED IN THIS PROJECT.

My cousin Fred Bredice attended your Camp Graylag for two summers and he said Sharman was a guest one year and he made fifty straight foul shots, missed one and then made 49 more. Again, it was the way he did it that must be able to be seen, even if you only showed three shots that could be kinesthetically studied.

Of course, if you are willing to take on such a project, getting the footage, and begin cutting and splicing the magnificent spots, which it would take someone like you to determine, you would have to be able to get your hands on the footage.

THIS IS WHERE I WANT YOU TO START. Another of your students, Al Vestro Junior (you knew him and his father as he attended Camp Graylag for two summers) refuses to part with all the reel to reel tapes of Billy Finn (including the 52 point game in which he did things beyond human imagination which I attempted to write about but I am certain only gives you the tip of the iceberg) (or any of them for that matter.) AS A CLINICAL PSYCHOLOGIST WHO WAS A LIFELONG FRIEND OF BOTH AL VESTRO AND BILLY FINN, I WOULD SAY THIS HAS TO DO WITH ENVY, HATRED AND THE FACT THAT BILLY FINN'S VERY EXISTENCE PREVENTED ALLIE VESTRO IN HIS OWN MIND FROM FULFILLING HIS FATHER'S DREAM ABOUT HIM ACCOMPLISHING WHAT BILLY FINN WAS ACTUALLY ABLE TO DO. WHILE THAT WOULD BE ONE HELLUVA BURDEN FOR ANY KID TO HAVE TO DEAL WITH, IT IS NEVERTHELESS STUCK IN HIS UNCONSCIOUS AS IF IT WERE YESTERDAY. IT IS PERHAPS OUT OF RESPECT FOR YOU, "BOB COUSY" THAT AL VESTRO MIGHT RECONSIDER.

I would recommend you telephone him to discuss this matter and then get back to me regarding how you feel about the entire idea. I have also enclosed some reviews of my work as a psychologist, articles I have written et. al.

I made it a point to study with the best in whatever I did In trumpet I studied with Frank Szabo who played lead for Count Basie and Buddy Rich among others. In high school everyone knew that all Frank was ever going to do was play trumpet, so Harry James drafted him to play third trumpet on the road for his last two years of high school, for which he got full credit. HAD BILLY FINN BEEN ALLOWED TO GO PRO AFTER HIGH SCHOOL, OR PERHAPS HAVE HAD A PROGRAM WHERE YOU WERE HIS MENTOR FOR THE LAST TWO YEARS OF HIGH SCHOOL, HE WOULD BE ALIVE TODAY! Al Vestro's cell phone # is 203 910-5010.

cc: Barbara DeLuca   Respectfully Requested,
(sent the newsclipping to Billy Finn 50 years old)

Len Bergantino, Ed.D., Ph.D.

BILLY FINN WAS THE BEST BASKETBALL PLAYER THAT EVER LIVED!

There are a few problems with this statement from your point of view. The first is "Who the hell is Billy Finn?" and the second is "Who the hell am I to make the statement?" THE THIRD IS THE MOST IMPORTANT FOR ME IN THAT WHAT HE DID WITH A BASKETBALL I NEVER SAW BEFORE BILLY FINN AND I NEVER SAW AFTER BILLY FINN! He painted a Picasso every time he touched a basketball. Often he was victimized by the perceptions of "ordinary people" and when these "ordinary people" were basketball coaches although he achieved a level of recognition in his lifetime, he was prevented from achieving the full magnificence of his capability. IN OTHER WORDS THE ONLY WAY ONE COULD ADEQUATELY COACH BILLY FINN WOULD BE TO GIVE HIM THE BASKETBALL AND SAY, "BILLY, PAINT ME A PICASSO ON THE COURT AND DO WHATEVER YOU WANT WITH THE TEAM!" ANYTHING ELSE WOULD BE TO PUT HIM IN A STRAITJACKET!

From an ordinary person's point of view Billy Finn was the best high school basketball player of his time who died a tragic death in an automobile alcohol related death at the age of eighteen years old. He had the state record in Connecticut with 52 points until Calvin Murphy broke it with 60 points and eventually played pro basketball for the Houston Rockets. Billy Finn was more exciting sitting on the bench dribbling the ball between his legs without paying any attention to what he was doing than Calvin Murphy was with the Rockets!

I am compelled to write about Billy Finn who died when I was 18 years old, some fifty years ago. Since then given I lived and he did not I have had the opportunity to become Dr. Len Bergantino, a clinical psychologist of international acclaim and a musician who made a cd with world renown jazz guitarist Joe Diorio entitled "Falling In Love. I am told if you goggle lenbergantino.com there are 37,700 hits on the internet. In Australia my work was said to have "lasting theraeutic affect" and was "a kind of mental precision that electrified the Australian Therapeutic Community." In other words I have paranormal sensitivities and that is why I am attempting to give you some of the Picasso of what composed Billy Finn. At the Royal College of Medicine in London in 1992 I gave a workshop entitled "The Development And Use Of Extrasensory Perception In The Practice of Psychoanalysis, Psychotherapy and Clinical Hypnosis." Chances are I always had these abilities, even when I knew Billy Finn and played three hours of basketball with him on a daily basis for four years.

Billy Finn was capable of getting 52 points every game!!! He was the victim of a caste system known as the education of the times geared to the so called benefit of the masses and a family caste system where Billy Finn himself had little ability to evaluate how good he was. In his own mind he lived in the shadow of his older brother Allie Finn and saw himself as equal to his next older brother Mark Finn. Allie Finn became an M.D. and Mark Finn a dentist. The reality of the situation despite the family caste system was neither could hold a candle to the God given talents of baby brother Billy Finn. In other words if we look at the axiom "Give To Caesar What Is Caesars!" Billy Finn got screwed!

DEFINITION OF BASKETBALL AT THAT TIME

During Billy Finn's lifetime basketball was a game of finesse. Today's game of basketball is a game of brute strength, physical power, aggression, and as in the case of Kobe Bryant, an unconquerable spirit of doing what it takes to win!

The only one I can compare to Billy Finn was a baseball player, that cannot be judged by statistics alone. The most exciting baseball player I ever saw was Willie Mays in 1954 at the Polo Grounds - at that time known as "The Say Hey Kid!" He could catch a routine fly ball and you knew you were seeing something you never saw before and would never see again! Finn was like that!

The best pro basketball player I ever saw was Elgin Baylor in terms of what he could do with his body! And he did it first! The best pure shooters I ever saw were Bill Sharman and Larry Bird of the Boston Celtics. One game when the Celtics were playing the Lakers I saw Larry Bird make 18 straight shots from beyond the circle during warmups without hitting the rim, just net! The best hitter I ever saw was Ted Williams, when he was an old man fighting Mickey Mantle for the batting title. When Williams got up to bat in batting practice the entire ballpark stopped talking and you couldn't hear a pin drop. Williams hit the most vicious line drives off the Green Monster Fence at Fenway Park I have ever seen. They almost bounced back to second base! Billy Finn was like that! Bob Cousy met Billy Finn when he was in the eighth grade and said he had nothing to teach him. Cousy was the starting guard for the Boston Celtics that under Bill Russell won many NBA Championships. When Russell was the Center the Celtics won eleven titles in 13 years. Russell was the most dominating figure to play any pro sport.

About Billy Finn

1. Billy Finn's wrists were as big as my ankles. He had extra ordinary power in his wrists that enabled him to do much of what I have only seen by him.
2. Billy Finn was about 5 foot eleven inches tall and weighed approximately 165 pounds.
3. Billy Finn's hands were huge. He could palm a basketball which was unusual for a guy five ft. 11 inches. Bill Russell had huge hands.
4. Billy Finn had an overall perspective of all the players on the court and could position the other nine anywhere he wanted and with the power in his wrists always find the open man! The only other player-coach I ever saw who had this one skill was the then coach of the Los Angeles Lakers-Mike Dunleavy. It is hard to explain this one unless you experience it first hand.
5. Billy Finn had incredibly quick reflexes that were so far above the norm as to be thought to be almost inhuman.
6. When Billy Finn combined his reflexes with his wrists and a quick jerk motion with a leg to either side he was virtually uncheckable.
7. For example, when Carl Spencer used to check him (Carl was a talented tall center) at Fulton Park courts Billy would take him in the Center spot, backing in to a guy almost seven inches taller and like lighting use the wrist and the jerk to throw a hook shot from the left or the right side that was unstoppable, and Carl Spencer could play defense!
8. My cousin, Freddie Bredice was All state from Torrington averaging about 22 a game and later became Little All American from Springfield College. One Summer Is up games at Fulton Park with Spencer, Finn, Fred Bredice, and other excellent basketball players. Cousin Fred Bredice who had just graduated from Torrington as an All State basketball player said of Billy Finn,

who had just completed his freshman year of high school, "Where the hell did that kid Finn come from? Mars? He is unbelievable!"

9. Billy Finn used to drive into the deep corner, where great shooters today shoot jump shots from 3 point land in the corner, driving down either the left side or the right side, and on the left side with his left hand thrown hook shots that went clean through only hitting the net, not the rim and on the right side doing the same thing with his right hand. He used to hit these hook shots from the circle with either hand as well. I certainly have never seen that before or after Billy Finn! Have you! He was to basketball as MichaelAngelo was to the Cistine Chapel! I suppose he was born a professional basketball player. He just never got the chance to play with people who might have been close to being his peers. He admired Bob Cousy and Oscar Robertson a great deal!

10. The upside of playing with him for me was he moved all 9 players to one side of the court and hit me with five straight passes in the corner where I was all alone and I had ten points in two minutes. The downside was I had the awkward growing pains of a high school adolescent and one time he flicked his wrist from half court and the ball came at the speed of one of Sandy Koufax's fastballs and hit me right in the face all alone under the hoop for a layup. There was tremendous laughter at my predicament and within three minutes my replacement got hit in the face all alone under the hoop for a layup.

I was a baseball pitcher and when I tell you the ball traveled from half court with the flick of a wrist and hit me in the face at a faster velocity than my fastball, that was something I never saw before or after Billy Finn. When he played with the older guys such as Marty Sweeney, whom Finn admired, they did not get hit in the face with the ball and they played as a well oiled machine comparable to the smoothness of a Rolls Royce Engine.

I apologize that it has taken me fifty years to write this paper to attempt to give the reader a flavor of the once in a lifetime magnificence of the greatest basketball player I ever had the privilege to know. I am of the opinion that those in the future who have the opportunity to study any game films that might be made available will be able to enhance their own level of playing basketball. For example, I was always a great shooter but I was so slow that a good defender could stay right on top of me and I would not be able to get the shot off. Billy Finn in one evening took me down the jump, as if he was teaching an elephant to dance, had me learn two moves -one to the left and one to the right, to be put into action the second I noticed something in the defensive player and guaranteed to get me by them for a layup - at which point they would stop checking me as close as they did - and if they did I would do it again! At the time if you asked any reasonable basketball player if I could be taught to drive by people they would have said it was impossible! While Billy Finn and Muhammed Ali had something in common, that they were not that good passing academic examinations, as Ali flunked the army exam and when asked said, "I said I was the greatest! I didn't say I was the brightest!" In the case of Billy Finn, he was not only the greatest on the court but the brightest in terms of teaching a skill that would enhance that player's unique abilities!

March 12, 2012

DEAR BASKETBALL RE: PURCHASE OF BILLY FINN
LOVERS: 52 POINT GAME REEL TO REEL
                            FILM IN COLOR FROM AL VESTRO
                            FOR $1,000,000!!!!!!!!!!!!!!!!!!!!!!!!

There are certain persons with one of a kind abilities whose legacy belongs to the world after they are gone. Billy Finn was one of these such as Michaelangelo was to the Cistine Chapel, Enrico Caruson was to the Metropolitan Opera and Toscanini was to LA Scala and The NBC Orchestra in the 1950's. Their work transcends their generation.

My self and Bill Guisto (long time basketball afficionado and college referee) are in agreement having 50 years to consider the matter that Billy Finn was the best basketball player we ever had the privilege to witness, including high school, pro or college. When he was in the eighth grade Bob Cousy told him he had nothing to teach him! Guisto on occasion says Pete Maravich was his equal. John Gilmore comes out to Las Vegas to visit Bill Guisto to talk basketball frequently (Gilmore, regarded as basketball genius level)

BARBARA DE LUCA SENT ME THE ENCLOSED NEWSPAPER CLIPPINGS RE: BILLY FINN A FEW WEEKS AGO. AS I WAS A PALL BEARER AT HIS FUNERAL I COULD NOT BRING MYSELF TO READ THEM THE FIRST TIME AND AFTER TWO WEEKS I HAVE FINALLY READ THEM.

SACRED HEART IS ALWAYS RAISING MONEY! I PROPOSE A CITY WIDE MONEY RAISING AFFAIR IN WATERBURY TO RAISE ONE MILLION DOLLARS AND GIVE IT TO AL VESTRO TO PURCHASE THE BILLY FINN TAPE AND SACRED HEART BE GIVEN THE VIDEO (MADE FROM THE REEL TO REEL) AND THAT SAID COPIES BE SOLD FOR $500 A PIECE TO PLAYERS FROM THE NBA WHO WANT TO LEARN THE INTANGIBLE QUALITIES THAT GO INTO MAGNIFICENCE AS A BALL HANDLER!

BARBARA DE LUCA (FORMERLY BARBARA PARSONS) ADDRESS IS

22 Meadowbrook Drive Shelton, Connecticut 06484-2519. She has both the mental acuity and the depth of personhood to successfully manage such a campaign.

Of course, I will help in any way that I can.

Cordially,
Len Bergantino, Ed.D., Ph.D.,

June 29, 2012

Mr. Robert S. Cousy
427 Salisbury Street
Worcester, Mass. 04609-1266

DEAR "BOB COUSY":

I want you to help me with a variety of issues tangentially related to you, Camp Graylag and some of your students THAT IN MY HEART OF HEARTS I THINK AND FEEL ARE FUNDAMENTAL TO A TRANSMISSION OF THE CULTURE OF BASKETBALL AT IT'S HIGHEST LEVEL OF EXCELLENCE.

As were you at Holy Cross, I was trained by the Jesuits at Fairfield University receiving an M.A. prior to my doctoral work at the University of Southern California (Bill Sharman's School).

Throughout my four years of high school I had the honor of being professionally entertained by a daily magic show put on at the hands of Billy Finn (we played about four hours a day 1957-1961).

I am told that you know who he is in that you had him and his friend Luke McGinnis as guests in your home when he was in the seventh grade and you immediately sensed the natural talent of Billy Finn.

The reason you did not hear much more about him was a tragic occurrence where his life was ended prematurely right after high school in an automobile accident. I was a pall bearer at his funeral but did not have my personal mental equipment developed to any level where I could have pursued what I am doing now in terms of what I propose to you.

About five months ago, a former classmate of mine and Billy Finn, whom I reunited with at our fiftieth high school reunion, sent me the newspaper clippings of Billy Finn's death. I remember not reading it intentionally at the time because I was so emotionally distraught over the situation. I have enclosed a copy of that newspaper clipping as well as material I have written in retrospect as to why I thought he was great at any level of play, pro, college or high school and the way he got the fifty two points was the important matter, not the fifty two points. FOR EXAMPLE, WHEN YOU DID THINGS I HAVE NEVER SEEN BEFORE OR AFTER YOU DID THEM, THE ANNOUNCER WAS ALWAYS YELLING OUT "COUSY HAS PERIPHERAL VISION!"

I have seen a lot of people throw behind the back passes, but there is really no way to put in context UNLESS YOU SEE THE FILM CLIPS FOR YOURSELF, ON THE GOD GIVEN MIRACLES THAT YOU, BILLY FINN, AND I UNDERSTAND FROM A RELIABLE BASKETBALL REFEREE, PETE MARAVICH, WERE ABLE TO PERFORM OF A "MAGICAL NATURE" THAT MUST BE ABLE TO BE VIEWED FOR ALL TIME IN THE BASKETBALL HALL OF FAME!

While there is a Billy Finn award, only those who are over 65 ever got to see him play and others younger have no idea what he actually did, or what you actually did.

On a personal preference level I THINK THE GAME OF BASKETBALL WHEN YOU PLAYED WAS A FINESSE GAME AND IT WOULD ALSO BE IMPORTANT TO HAVE THE BODY MOVEMENTS OF ELGIN BAYLOR IN HIS LAST YEAR AT SEATTLE AND EARLY YEARS WITH THE MINNEAPOLIS LAKERS, AS WELL AS THE PURE SHOOTING OF YOUR CLOSE FRIEND AND COLLEAGUE BILL SHARMAN INCLUDED IN THIS PROJECT.

My cousin Fred Bredice attended your Camp Graylag for two summers and he said Sharman was a guest one year and he made fifty straight foul shots, missed one and then made 49 more. Again, it was the way he did it that must be able to be seen, even if you only showed three shots that could be kinesthetically studied.

Of course, if you are willing to take on such a project, getting the footage, and begin cutting and splicing the magnificent spots, which it would take someone like you to determine, you would have to be able to get your hands on the footage.

THIS IS WHERE I WANT YOU TO START. Another of your students, Al Vestro Junior (you knew him and his father as he attended Camp Graylag for two summers) refuses to part with all the reel to reel tapes of Billy Finn (including the 52 point game in which he did things beyond human imagination which I attempted to write about but I am certain only gives you the tip of the iceberg) (or any of them for that matter.) AS A CLINICAL PSYCHOLOGIST WHO WAS A LIFELONG FRIEND OF BOTH AL VESTRO AND BILLY FINN, I WOULD SAY THIS HAS TO DO WITH ENVY, HATRED AND THE FACT THAT BILLY FINN'S VERY EXISTENCE PREVENTED ALLIE VESTRO IN HIS OWN MIND FROM FULFILLING HIS FATHER'S

DREAM ABOUT HIM ACCOMPLISHING WHAT BILLY FINN WAS ACTUALLY ABLE TO DO. WHILE THAT WOULD BE ONE HELLUVA BURDEN FOR ANY KID TO HAVE TO DEAL WITH, IT IS NEVERTHELESS STUCK IN HIS UNCONSCIOUS AS IF IT WERE YESTERDAY. IT IS PERHAPS OUT OF RESPECT FOR YOU, "BOB COUSY" THAT AL VESTRO MIGHT RECONSIDER.

I would recommend you telephone him to discuss this matter and then get back to me regarding how you feel about the entire idea. I have also enclosed some reviews of my work as a psychologist, articles I have written et. al.

I made it a point to study with the best in whatever I did In trumpet I studied with Frank Szabo who played lead for Count Basie and Buddy Rich among others. In high school everyone knew that all Frank was ever going to do was play trumpet, so Harry James drafted him to play third trumpet on the road for his last two years of high school, for which he got full credit. HAD BILLY FINN BEEN ALLOWED TO GO PRO AFTER HIGH SCHOOL, OR PERHAPS HAVE HAD A PROGRAM WHERE YOU WERE HIS MENTOR FOR THE LAST TWO YEARS OF HIGH SCHOOL, HE WOULD BE ALIVE TODAY! Al Vestro's cell phone # is 203 910-5010.

cc: Barbara DeLuca   Respectfully Requested,
(sent the newspaper clipping to Billy 50 years old)
                                        Len Bergantino, Ed.D., Ph.D.

April 24, 2012

Dear John, (Gilmore- Elite Basketball Coach)

Thanks for writing back. I will be 69 years old. You are older than me. The problem is that Billy Finn's name and trophy will be famous but unless you saw Jimmy Piersall jump over that right field wall and rob Yogi of the home run or you saw him do the same to someone when he brought his barnstormers to Waterbury, you have no idea of just how great he was as an outfielder. With Finn, there is no way to adequately describe what you describe as magical because I never saw anybody do it before or after him.

When I taught at Wilby in 1967-68 Jack had me coaching freshman basketball. I remember we were four wins no losses and I enjoyed it, but I did not know enough to progress as a basketball coach I was a shooter, plain and simple! On the other hand I would have advanced quite well as a baseball coach if I had chosen to do so. I know that game inside out.

Jack Delaney, SHoes Granato, Mario Ciarlo and myself used to go up to Mayo's after every Wilby High School basketball game and I had clams and beer. Jack always dominated the conversation as he knew more about basketball than any of us and he always ended with the same argument - a winner - that Bill Russell was the most dominating figure to play any professional sport in that he won 11 out of 13 world championships. After Jack won that one it was time to go home and get ready for another day at Wilby. Artie Williams played then.

In Billy's back yard I beat him 11-0 one summer afternoon. He had a blue backboard. I threw in 11 35 foot jumpers. He said "I am going to deny it. No one will ever believe you did it!" Our relationship was like that, you know how kids always break each others balls at that age. I hung out with him every day of high school and then he wasn't there any more. A LIFETIME LOSS FOR CERTAIN!

Al Vestro will not part with reel to reel some in color tapes of Billy Finn -including the 52 point game. I THINK WATERBURY SHOULD BUILD A LITTLE CONCRETE VIDEO CENTER ON THE GREEN AS A MONUMENT TO WATERBURY'S GREATEST ATHLETE EVER AND CHARGE MONEY TO SEE THOSE TAPES.

Waterbury newspapers won't print anything I write despite the fact I have eighty publications and a book that was a master classic in the field of psychotherapy.

Sincerely
Len

April 25, 2012

FACTS RE: PEOPLE WHO ACTUALLY SAW BILLY FINN PLAY BASKETBALL!.

1. John Gilmore -elite Waterbury Basketball Coach described Finn as "MAGICAL".
2. Billy Guisto -high school and sometime college basketball referee "Billy Finn was the best who ever played the game!"
3. Len Bergantino, Ed.D., Ph.D. -former freshman basketball coach under Head Coach Jack Delaney who coached Billy Finn- "Billy Finn was the best basketball player that ever lived - pro-college or high school. I have never seen what he did with a ball before him or after him. WHILE AT SACRED HEART HIGH SCHOOL WE WERE THINKING OF DESCRIBING EVENTS IN TERMS OF B.C. AND A.D. AS FAR AS BASKETBALL GOES IT IS "B.F. AND A.F. - BEFORE BILLY FINN AND AFTER BILLY FINN!"
4. BOB COUSY HAD NOTHING TO TEACH HIM IN THE SEVENTH GRADE! THAT OUGHT TO TELL YOU SOMETHING! (BOSTON CELTICS -Holy Cross All American-1954).
5. Barry Rabinowitz -professional sports photographer in a conversation two weeks ago from his daughter's villa in Rome, Italy. "You will never guess who I got an e-mail from sending me pictures of the ten most influential people she ever met - Lynn LeBon (she and Barry were three years younger than Billy Finn from Waterbury) AND ONE OF THOSE PICTURES WAS OF BILLY FINN.
6. Barbara Parsons DeLuca thought enough of Billy Finn to save and send me the original Waterbury Republican Newspaper clippings after his death.
7. George O'Meara, deceased basketball afficionado and the best among mortals at Fulton Park Court where he had his ashes distributed after his death by his children, survived by a daughter and two sons, informed me "EVERY DAY OF GEORGE O'MEARA'S LIFE HE TALKED ABOUT BILLY FINN!"

RECOMMENDATION: WATERBURY REPUBLICAN, CITY OF WATERBURY AND SACRED HEART HIGH SCHOOL GET TOGETHER AND BUILD A SHRINE WHERE HIS BODY OF WORK CAN BE SEEN FOR THE FUTURE SO ONE WILL NOT HAVE TO REINVENT THE WHEEL. CALLED "A TRANSMISSION OF THE CULTURE!"

Sincerely,
Len Bergantino, B.A., M.A., MS. ED., ED.D., PH.D., ABPP

submitted by Len Bergantino, Ed.D., Ph.D., ABPP
CLINICAL PSYCHOLOGIST IN CA, AZ & HI 310 207-9397

THE DAY I GOT EVEN WITH BILLY FINN!

I am a clinical psychologist writing about nuances that occurred fifty years ago that were not apparent to either myself or Billy Finn at the time they occurred. Billy Finn was my best friend throughout four years of high school. I never got mad at him and he never got mad at me. He was the best basketball player I ever saw at any level and he was my mentor at that game. I was always a great shooter but without Billy Finn teaching me how to drive by even the fastest defender given I used to be called snow shoes by my grammar school baseball coach, and without cousin Little All American Fred Bredice teaching me to shoot the jump shot quickly with the emphasis on getting it off quickly instead of the height of the jump, the next forty years would have been very different for me athletically.

TOTAL HUMILIATION

In the early 1970's Eric Berne, M.D. wrote a book called GAMES PEOPLE PLAY. "Total Humiliation" was not one of them but as I looked upon what Billy Finn and I enjoyed doing this was the name of the game. He had gotten me twice. I was the most authentic guy in the high school, but Billy Finn could lie better than I could tell the truth and everyone would believe him. He got me twice. First he convinced the entire school of an event that never happened, telling them I snuck up into his sister's room in the middle of the night as a prowler might do; and second, he denied that I beat him 11-0 making eleven straight jump shots.

It was somewhere near the beginning of basketball season and Johnny Egan who played guard for Providence College in 1960 (along with Lenny

Wilkens) invited the entire high school basketball team down to Providence College to see the game as a courtesy to Billy Finn.

As people use models of those who have gone before them so it was with Bob Cousy (guard for the Boston Celtics who told Billy Finn in the seventh grade he had nothing to teach him) and Johnny Egan from Hartford Weaver High School who was known as a pretty fancy ballhandler. Egan wound up playing for the Los Angeles Lakers for a couple of years in the late sixties. Billy Finn saw Johnny Egan drive toward the hoop and wrap his right arm completely around his body throwing a pass that hit the open man on the way to the hoop for a layup and no matter how hard Billy tried he could never quite get that one down, but it became the basis of his idealization of Johnny Egan.

JOHNNY EGAN COMES TO VISIT OUR TEAM

Egan walked in the room and I do not know what possessed him to walk up to me and say, "WHAT DO YOU THINK OF ME?" Perhaps he noticed that Billy Finn and I were talking and we were close pals. AS SOON AS HE ASKED THE QUESTION I SAW THE HORROR ON FINN'S FACE AND HE AND I BOTH KNEW IT WAS PAYBACK TIME. I LOOKED JOHNNY EGAN RIGHT IN THE EYE AND OUT IT CAME AS IF SHOT OUT OF A CANNON, "YOU CAN'T SHOOT!" Egan went ballistic. He demanded to play me one on one in front of the entire Providence College crowd before the game. Finn knew that against me one on one if you missed three shots the game was over, so I said to Egan, "Let's do it! I am going to whip your ass in front of two thousand people!" This went on for awhile and finally two of Egan's teammates had to restrain him as they both grabbed him from behind and dragged him out of the hotel room doorway. THE LAST I EVER SAW OF JOHNNY EGAN WERE HIS HEELS SCRAPING THE FLOOR AS HE WAS DRAGGED AWAY!

<u>TO PLAY TOTAL HUMILIATION TOOK BOTH</u> <u>COURAGE AND GENIUS</u>

I make a point of this because Billy Finn did not apply himself academically and people might underestimate his brilliance. As a basketball instinctual player he had no equal. In other words his intelligence quotient was off the charts. Perhaps Yogi Berra's 1947 conversation with Yankee Manager Bucky Harris can be used as an example. Berra was told to go up to the plate and think while he was hitting. He struck out on three straight pitches and came back and said "How the hell can I think and hit at the same time!" Well, Billy Finn was Pure Being In Action. There was no gap between thought and movement. He was all one at all times as in pure being with a basketball in his hands.

Second, academically I lived longer than Billy Finn and was able to get two doctorates, two masters and a baccalaureate degree. Yet, Billy Finn beat me twice at this game and I only beat him once; and it was the sort of game you had to be ready alert to never make a mistake, lest the entire high school haze you for a couple of months at a time. SO IT TOOK A CERTAIN KIND OF GENIUS AT GAMESMANSHIP AND COURAGE AS IT WAS NOT A GAME FOR THE FEINT OF HEART!

WHY I NEVER GOT MAD AT BILLY FINN

is sometimes a mystery even to me as he did some things that if anybody else did they would be looking for their Sunday teeth on the front lawn. He would put one over on me and "dumb down", that is make his face look not as smart as he was, while looking at the ground, and saying in an embarrased manner "HEY BERG! (which meant "I got you this time, you bastard!") At the same time he did this he would some how reach in and touch my heart, so I immediately forgave him and saw the humor from his point of view! I LOVED BILLY FINN!

The Reincarnated
Soul of Billy Finn

If you read my other books you will see that I
have lived my life as "a holy man" and made a deal
with "the holy spirit" around 1980. While this is not a story
for this book part of the gift I was given was to have sometimes one and
sometime repetitive glimpses of someone I knew IN VERY PRECISE
DETAIL WITH A CHARACTERISTIC OR TWO THAT I HAVE
ONLY SEEN IN THAT ONE PERSON OVER THE COURSE OF MY
SEVENTY SIX YEAR OLD LIFETIME, only to have it flashed back
to me in a WAY THAT I KNOW WITH PRIMITIVE CERTAINTY
THAT I AS IN THIS CASE HAVE SEEN THE REINCARNATED
SOUL OF BILLY FINN REAPPEAR SOME THIRTY THREE
YEARS AFTER HIS DEATH.

IN THE CASE OF BILLY FINN THE REINCARNATED SOUL
OF BILLY FINN WAS REBORN IN THE BODY AND TALENT OF
LOS ANGELES LAKERS COACH AND LOS ANGELES CLIPPERS
COACH MIKE DUNLEAVY.

WHAT THIS MEANS IS THAT GOD GAVE BILLY FINN A
SECOND CHANCE BECAUSE THE WORLD BLOCKED HIM
THE FIRST TIME!

Jerry West got Kobe Bryant right out of high school to play professional
basketball. The same happened for Lebron James. When Billy Finn was in
high school NCAA rules insisted one had to go to college prior to playing
professional basketball. I am certain this had a deleterious effect on many
who would have been great professional basketball players, who for one
reason or another either were not cut out for college or had little interest in

college. While Billy Finn knew more about basketball than anyone I ever met he didn't care much about academics at Sacred Heart High School. Yet, without the money Finn raised there might not be a Sacred Heart High School!

Xlibris

BERGEN-BELSEN
1940
BIS
1945
GERMANS – JEWS – HOLOCAUSTS
and
THE COLLECTIVE UNCONSCIOUS
DR. LEN BERGANTINO, Ed.D., Ph.D.

Xlibris

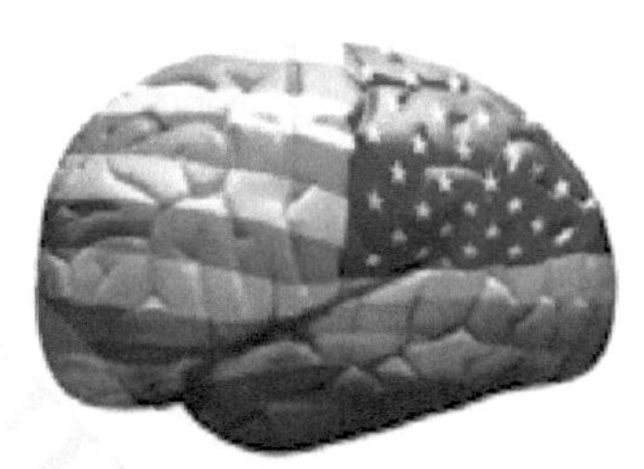

POLITICAL PSYCHOLOGY
INVASIONS

DR. LEN BERGANTINO, Ed.D., Ph.D.

When Baseball was King
The New York Yankees were
King of Baseball
Dr. Len Bergantino, Ed.D., Ph.D.

RoseDog Books

The Reverend Dr. Len Bergantino, Ed.D., Ph.D.

From 1962 through 2008, Len Bergantino began each day with pro bono writings and invasive interventions that honor and expand upon the first amendment rights of United States citizens. In all areas, he is both knowledgeable and finds national, state, and local governments are stuck in socially unsolvable positions. He created ways to invade entire cultures and governments to move them stuck in quicksand off the dime and into a society that spirals upward. He refers to the creation of these methods as sanctimonious psychoproctological invasions in the creation of a political psychology that should be studied by all human beings who want to make a difference and give meaning to their lives.

Sanctimonious Psychoproctological Invasions: The Handbook for Political Analysis

Len Bergantino is a multi-faceted individual who achieved international prominence in the areas of psychoanalysis, psychotherapy, clinical psychology, and music. His other fields include education and religion, with a precautionary knowledge of medicine and law. He is a swashbuckler in terms of knowing the right thing to do and has the temperament of a The Guerrero in getting it done!

The Reverend Dr. Len Bergantino, Ed.D. (USC), Ph.D., D. Div. Political Analyst

From 2012 through 2018, Leo Bergantino began each day with pro bono writings and invasive interventions that insist and expand upon the first amendment rights of United States citizens. In all areas, he is both knowledgeable and feels national, state, and local governments are stuck in socially immobile positions. He created ways to invade entire cultures and governments to move those stuck in quicksand off the dime and into a society that spirals upward. He refers to the creation of these methods as sanctimonious psychoprocratological invasions in the creation of a political psychology that should be studies by all human beings who want to make a difference and give meaning to their lives.

About the Author

Leo Bergantino is a multi-faceted individual who achieved international prominence in the areas of psychoanalysis, psychotherapy, clinical psychology, and music. His other fields include education and religion, with a precarious knowledge of medicine and law. He is a weathervane in terms of knowing the right thing to do and has the temperament of Che Guevara in getting it done!

ISBN: 978-1-955-691-54-3 • $xx.xx

ROSEDOG BOOKS
585 Alpha Dr, Pittsburgh, PA 15238

THE REVEREND
DR. LEN BERGANTINO, ED. D, PH.D.

The Sanctimonious
Psychoproctological Invasions

THE HANDBOOK FOR POLITICAL ANALYSIS

DR. LEN BERGANTINO, ED. D. (USC) PH.D., D. DIV.
POLITICAL ANALYST

DR. LEN BERGANTINO, ED.D., PH.D.

BOOK COLLECTIONS

Books that are either published or will be published authored by **Dr. Len Bergantino** as these books were written as the thing-in itself and were divinely inspired by the Holy Spirit to at the very least give men and women an opportunity to be more fully themselves and more in touch with their own nature. It is strongly recommended that the readers develop their level of attention to read all four books and permit them to become part parcel of how each individual answers the question "TO BE OR NOT TO BE". As The Reverend Dr. Len Bergantino is seventy five years old, he will not be around personally to do psychoanalysis or psychotherapy with you, therefore these books were written on the basis of them being around for at least TWO HUNDRED YEARS!!!

1. I AM FREUD! Psychoanalysis Is the Only Method of Cure: It's Too Bad No One Knows How to Do One!!!
2. Reverse Analysis, the Existential Shift, Gestalt Family Therapy and the Prevention of the Next Holocaust
3. The Art of Psychotherapy and the Liberation of the Therapist
4. The Essence of Music
5. When Baseball was King The New York Yankees were King of Baseball
6. Germans – Jews – Holocausts and the Collective Unconscious
7. Political Psychology Invasions
8. The Sanctimonious Psychoproctological Invasions: The Handbook for Political Analysis
9. The Denial of Reverse Racism in America
10. The Greatest Basketball Player I Ever Saw

Letter from Pope Francis

Dr. LEN BERGANTINO, Ed.D.(USC), Ph.D., A.B.P.P.

Psychoanalysis

(424) 293-9511

Dear Billionaire,

I WANT YOU TO GIVE A GIFT OF ABOUT TWO MILLION DOLLARS
AS A TAX WRITEOFF MUCH AS STIPENDS WERE GIVEN TO
MICHAELANGELO FOR PAINTING THE CISTINE CHAPEL!
ALONG WITH THIS GIFT AS MY BENEFACTOR IT IS PARAMOUNT THAT
YOU FIND THE BEST SYSTEM THAT MARKETS AND DISTRIBUTES BOOKS
AND GIVE THEM WHATEVER THEY WANT TO PUT IN BOOKSTORES OR
DISPLAY SIX BOOKS I HAVE PUBLISHED BETWEEN NOVEMBER, 2016
AND DECEMBER, 2019.

While it is testamount to PROVING THE EXISTENCE OF GOD
ANY AND ALL BOOKS WILL BE SHIPPED TO YOU UPON REQUEST FOR THIS
TAX WRITEOFF!!! (UP TO SIX BOOKS FOR DONOR EVALUATION PURPOSES)

MY BOOKS ARE A PUBLIC SERVICE IN THAT THEY WILL TURN
A DOWNWARD SPIRALING SOCIETY INTO AN U_PWARD SPIRALING
SOCIETY WHEN READ AN INGESTED IN TOTO!

The pages that follow give the billionaire of front and
back book covers of how one can develop and utilize "HIGHER
SENSE PERCEPTION IN THE DEVELOPMENT OF LIFE PURSUITS TO BE ANY
FORM!!!
LEST THERE REMAIN A DEARTH OF QUALITY AND EXCELLENCE THE TAX
WRITEOFF OF THE BILLIONAIRE WILL PROVIDE A DEVELOPMENT IN
THE HIGHEST CALIBRE OF PERSONS AND CITIZENS FOR AT LEAST THE
NEXT TWO HUNDRED YEARS!!! PLEASE READ ON AND CALL BY LETTING
424-293-9511 RING TEN TIMES TO LEAVE A MESSAGE WITH A CALL BACK #!

Sincerely,

Dr. Len Bergantino, Ed.D., Ph.D.

1215 Brockton Ave., Ste. 104, W. Los Angeles, CA 90025-U.S.A.

Dr. LEN BERGANTINO, Ed.D.(USC), Ph.D., A.B.P.P.

Psychoanalysis

(424) 293-9511

November 21, 2019

Dear Psychoanalyst,

I want you to be on the lookout for a book recently sent by my
publisher entitled I AM FREUD! PSYCHOANALYSIS IS THE ONLY
METHOD OF CURE! IT'S TOO BAD NO ONE KNOWS HOW TO DO ONE!!!

THIS BOOK AND OTHERS I HAVE WRITTEN WILL HELP PSYCHOANALYSTS
BECOME "HIGHER SENSITIVES" (as written about in a book in 1967
by Shaffica Karagulla, DeVorss Press). This will make all the
difference in successfully working through transferences.

My first book, PSYCHOTHERAPY, INSIGHT AND STYLE: THE EXISTENTIAL
MOMENT, 1981 Allyn & Bacon, 1984 retitled MAKING AN IMPACT IN
THERAPY: HOW MASTER CLINICIANS INTERVIEW, Jason Aronson, Inc.
is an important preface in that the psychoanalytic chapter
actually has interviews with the best of Wilfred Bion"s
Analysands-Supervising and Training Analysts - M.D.'s as well
as the order in which Bion"s books must be read to develop
the level of attention required for psychoanalysis to, in
"good faith" continue to grow as a profession! Analysts
thought Bion"s work was brilliant conceptually and theoretically
but not relevant to the practice of psychoanalysis. This
 IS NOT TRUE AND I AM FREUD. THE BOOK IT TOOK ME FORTY YEARS
 TO WRITE, DEMONSTRATES MANY OF HIS UNIQUE TECHNICAL APPROACHES
 TIED TO THE QUALITY OF BEING OF THE PSYCHOANALYST.

FURTHER, BION SAID "THE ENTIRE PSYCHOANALYTIC LIBRARY IS GOOD
for about the first hour and one half of an Analysis! After that
YOU HAVE TO KNOW WHAT TO SAY TO THE PATIENT!" Martin Grotjahn,MD
told me "Psychoanalysis is a great method of education, but it
is ineffective as a method of treatment!"

My also new book "The Art of Psychotherapy And The Liberation of
The Therapist" remedies both the concerns of Bion and Grotjahn!
As I was trained by 17 or more world renown psychiatrists,
psychoanalysts and clinical psychologists THIS UPDATED VERSION
OF FORTY YEARS OF THE EXISTENTIAL MOMENT PROVIDES BOTH OPTIONS
OF WHAT YOU SAY TO A PATIENT THAT MUST BE INCORPORATED INTO
PSYCHOANALYTIC EDUCATION IN WAYS THAT PROVIDE EFFECTIVE
TREATMENT!   LOOK AT IT THIS WAY! FOR $300,000 OVER A 7 YEAR
PERIOD OF FIVE DAY A WEEK ANALYSIS THE PATIENT HAS A RIGHT TO
COME OUT OF THE ANALYSIS NOT AS CRAZY AS THE DAY THEY WENT IN!

Sincerely,

P.S.   I AM THE ONLY ONE WHO COULD ACTUALLY DO ALL OF WHAT WILFRED BION WROTE!
Dr. Len Bergantino, Ed.D. (USC), Ph.D.,A.B.P.P.

1215 Brockton Ave., Ste. 104, W. Los Angeles, CA 90025-U.S.A.

LEN BERGANTINO, Ed.D., Ph.D., A.B.P.P.

Psychoanalysis
(310) 207-9397

Clinical Psychologist

A.B.P.P. – Diplomate in Family Psychology
American Board of Professional Psychology

DO YOU THINK THAT SOME SLUG WHO LOOKS VERY PROFESSIONAL, WHO "WHISPERS" AN OCCASIONAL INTERPRETATION TO YOU FIVE TIMES A WEEK FOR 7 YEARS CAN MAKE ONE BIT OF DIFFERENCE IN YOUR LIFE OR DOES SUCH A PSYCHOTOXIC SLUG CALLED A PSYCHOANALYST MERELY STICK YOU IN AN EMOTIONAL TOILET BOWL FOR SEVEN YEARS HAVING THE CUMULATIVE RESULT OF TURNING YOU INTO A HOPELESS BASTARD WHO WILL NEVER TURN THE TRAGIC CORNER IN HIS OR HER LIFE?

CAN YOUR ANALYST ANALYZE AN ARCHAIC LIQUID SYMBIOTIC OR AN OSMOTIC TRANSFERENCE, OR CAN THEY EVEN RECOGNIZE THIS PHENOMENA IN ORDER TO ANALYZE IT.?! IF THE PSYCHANALYST CANNOT ANALYZE THESE TRANSFERENCES THEY CAN'T DO AN ANALYSIS!!!

I USED TO GET "GOOD FAITH" PATIENTS WHO HAD THE BALLS TO WORK ON THE CUTTING EDGE AT THE SAME TIME I DID BECAUSE THEY HAD HAD COMBINATIONS OF TWENTY YEARS OF TWO SEVEN YEAR ANALYSES PLUS SEVERAL BRIEFER PSYCHOTHERAPIES, ONLY TO BE AS CRAZY AS THE DAY THEY WALKED IN!!! (~$200,000.00)

AS DR. DONALD RINSLEY, M.D., FELLOW-AMERICAN COLLEGE OF PSYCHOANALYSTS WROTE ABOUT ME, MY WORK HAS BOTH A HEALING EFFECT AND AFFECT. PATIENTS USED TO PAY ME SIX MONTHS IN ADVANCE TO HOLD THE TIME OPEN BECAUSE I WAS IRREPLACEABLE. I WAS THE ONLY ONE WHO COULD ANALYZE THE PSYCHOTIC CORE OF THE PERSONALITY AND I WAS THE ONLY ONE WHO COULD ACTUALLY DO WHAT DR. WILFRED R. BION, MRCS (MEDICAL ROYAL COLLEGE OF SURGEONS) WROTE ABOUT ANALYZING THE PSYCHOTIC CORE OF THE PERSONALITY.

AS I AM SEVENTY SIX YEARS OLD, I HAVE WRITTEN FIVE BOOKS THAT MUST BE READ AND DIGESTED IN THEIR ENTIRETY. AS THESE BOOKS ARE THE THING-IN-ITSELF THEY WILL TRANSFORM THE READER INTO THE KINDS OF ANALYST, PATIENT AND PSYCHOTHERAPIST WHO CAN MAKE A DIFFERENCE IN HELPING PEOPLE TURN THE TRAGIC CORNER IN THEIR LIVES! IN OTHER WORDS, THESE FIVE BOOKS ARE ANALYSIS!

THESE BOOKS WERE WRITTEN TO BE AROUND FOR A FEW HUNDRED YEARS AND WERE DIRECTLY GUIDED BY THE ALMIGHTY!!

From the Vatican, 17 June 2019

Dear Mr Bergantino,

His Holiness Pope Francis has received your letter, and he has asked me to thank you.

The Holy Father will remember you in his prayers, and he invokes upon you God's blessings of joy and peace.

Yours sincerely,

Monsignor Paolo Borgia
Assessor

Mr Len Bergantino
1215 Brockton Avenue
Suite 104
Los Angeles, CA 90025
USA

Dr. Len Bergantino, Ed.D., Ph.D.

The Reverend Dr. Len Bergantino was trained in psychoanalysis including the paranormal and ordinary methods of training by Dr. Wilfred R. Biom. MCRS- Medical Royal College of Surgeons. Many of Bion's M.D. Analysands in Beverly Hills, CA, Dr. Martin Grotjahn, M.D. and Dr. Bruno Bettelheim, Ph.D. who was in Freud's original training group. They were all Training Analysts. Dr. Michael Paul M.D. is one of the two best of Bion's Training Analysands.

Dr. Donald Rinsley M.D., Fellow American College of Psychoanalysts wrote about me, "There is no doubt that some people possess a healing capacity and that others do not". "Envies ——jelousies — outsiderism".

A Review

By DONALD B. RINSLEY, M.D., F.R.S.H.,
Fellow, American College of Psychoanalysts;
Fellow, American Psychiatric Association

Psychotherapy, Insight and Style.
By Len Bergantino, Ed.D., Ph.D.
Boston: Allyn and Bacon, 1981, 288 pp.
Published in Bulletin of the Menninger Clinic,
Vol. 47, No. 5, September 1983.

There is no doubt that some people possess a healing capacity and that others do not; nor is there any doubt that a Zulu witch doctor, a Puerto Rican curandero, a Navaho medicine man or a voodoo spiritist may remit symptoms more effectively than the best trained psychotherapist or psychoanalyst. The differences between healing and therapy are not inconspicuous even as both may readily dissolve into quackery in the hands of the exploitive and the unscrupulous. A wise Freud once commented that the function of psychoanalysis is to convert neurotic misery into ordinary human suffering, a point of view to be dismissed only at one's peril even though it doubtless reflected the essence of Freud's depressive personality. From such few considerations as these emerge questions concerning the differences separating healing and therapy, the features that unite them and the goals and objectives they may be noted to share. And whatever answers to these questions may satisfy those who propound them will reflect whether one's Weltanschauung considers the world to be a vale of tears or, after the fashion of the Gallic optimist, Coué, a place where everything keeps getting better and better.

Veterans
Administration

1 July 1985   In Reply Refer To:

Len Bergantino, Ed.D., Ph.D.
10266 Kilronney Avenue
Los Angeles, California 90064

Dear Len:

How nice to receive yours of June 24th, and to learn of your upward spiral! I'm very pleased indeed to believe that my little review of your book has contributed to your success!

Frankly, Len, I have long been eructatively fed up with the sort of territorial cupidities and other evidences of narcissistic nonsensicality so many of the colleagues display. Such antics reveal the essentially limbic nature of people as it comes to be expressed in envies and jealousies to which you allude in your letter. When I read your book I knew at once of your outsider-ism (cf. Colin Wilson's seminal book of the same name—The Outsider) as well as your talent; since I know I am good also, I do not need to do the Big-Daddy-in-Cat-On-A-Hot-Tin-Roof bit, viz., to shit on one's sons out of envy and fear that they will appropriate my penis-cum-wife-cum-everything-else!

I trust your family are in good health. Keep in touch.

Most sincerely,

Donald B. Rinsley, M.D., F.R.S.H. (Lond.)
Associate Chief for Education
Psychiatry Service

Clinical Professor of Psychiatry
University of Kansas School of Medicine
Kansas City

DBR:mtf

The Books

I AM FREUD! Psychoanalysis Is the Only Method of Cure:

It's Too Bad No One Knows How to Do One!!!

This is a book for all time. As I had extrasensory perception to help me find out things on a primitive level and depth with an ability to pick up split-off, severe pathological projective identifications moment to moment in an era when psychologists were only permitted to be research psychoanalysts by the American Psychoanalytic Association (but tightly controlled where that research was going that in many ways nullified it as true psychoanalytic research), I present to you a book that might at that time have been considered wild psychoanalysis. And I will show you how extrasensory perception can be developed and utilized by the therapeutic use of self within the psychoanalytic frame in ways that can enhance the treatment of borderline, narcissistic, obsessive-compulsive, and schizophrenic disorders and other diagnoses, as well as help pinpoint psychophysiological awareness, which through the repetition compulsion, can prevent disease and will circumvent disease in later life. This kind of psychoanalysis will go a long way in preventing the next holocoust!

ORDER A COPY NOW!

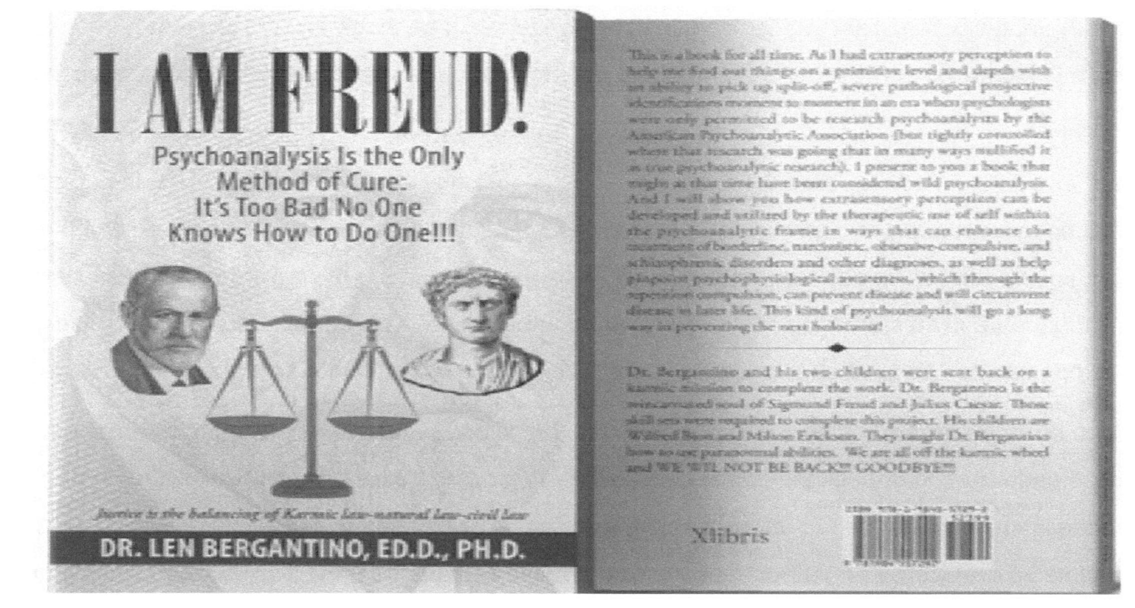

I DARED TO DISTURB THE UNIVERSE!!!

Dr. Len Bergantino Ed. D., Ph.D., releases 'I AM Freud! Psychoanalysis Is the Only Method of Cure: It's Too Bad No One Knows How to Do One!!!"

BEVERLY HILLS, Calif. – Dr. Len Bergantino, Ed.D., Ph.D., is the reincarnated soul of Sigmund Freud and Julius Caesar and his children Lisa Francesca is the reincarnated soul of the great British psychoanalyst Wilfred R. Bion and Cleopatra while his developmentally delayed son Alexander Leonardo is the reincarnated soul of Milton H. Erickson, M.D. (known as the father of Modern Medical Hypnosis and for Uncommon Therapy) and Decimus Brutus. All of those skill sets were necessary in the writing of "I Am Freud! Psychoanalysis Is the Only Method of Cure: It's Too Bad No One Knows How to Do One!!!" (published by Xlibris) and the issues it is meant to deal with at both conscious and unconscious levels.

Furthur, Bergantino in 1980, made a direct contact with God to have Bion and Erickson sent back as the reincarnated souls of his children to teach him what to do with the paranormal gifts that were given to him and unleashed by Erickson. Through this development, he, with God's tutelage became the best psychoanalyst that ever lived and began to implement Freud's plan that both psychoanalysis and subsequently developed psychotherapies would create the kind of patients who would and could then go out and create an upward spiraling society.

Wilhelm Reich, M.D. – Freud's most gifted training analyst said "If you can't do politics, you can't do analysis!" The book shows how to develop extrasensory perception so that analysts and therapists have an opportunity to develop the tools necessary to do the jobs at hand if they are so inclined. In this way, people will not pay for a five day a week, seven year analysis and come out as crazy as the day they began with few if any tools to carry on the work. "When I did an analysis with the crème de la crème of society, they customarily tripled their income and the quality of their life! (Don't waste $50,000 per year or $350,000 per analysis)."

The book is not based on anything Bergantino may or may not believe. It is based on his attaining a level of "pure being" that Jean Paul Sartre wrote about as the thing-in-itself. And it is at that level that this book was written as the thing-in-itself to effect change in the reader.

"I Am Freud! Psychoanalysis Is the Only Method of Cure: It's Too Bad No One Knows How to Do One!!!"

By Dr. Len Bergantino, Ed.D., Ph.D.

Hardcover | 6 x 9in | 504 pages | ISBN 9781984557308

Softcover | 6 x 9in | 504 pages | ISBN 9781984557292

E-Book | 504 pages | ISBN 9781984557285

Available at www.amazon.com and www.barnesandnoble.com

About the Author

Dr. Len Bergantino, Ed.D., Ph.D. practiced psychoanalysis in Beverly Hills, California from 1979-1991. He saw seven patients five days a week for between five and seven years totaling 49 hours a week and saw an occasional family therapy or clinical hypnosis case totaling 52 hours a week at $125 per hour; $625 per week; $240,000 per year. In addition, he trained psychiatrists and clinical psychologists at the international level delivering on his workshop promise "The Therapheutic Wizardry of Dr. Len Bergantino" at Wentworth Castle in Sheffield, England and training the British at the Royal College of Medicine in London in "Developing the Use of Extrasensory Perception in the Practice of Psychoanalysis, Psychotherapy and Clinical Hypnosis." In Brisbane, Australia, his work was described as "a kind of mental precision" that electrified the Australian Therapeutic Community and had lasting therapeutic impact. Furthermore, he was an affiliate of the Italian American Lawyers Association for seven years. He became an expert witness in both severe parental Alienation Syndrome in criminal cases. He was the only clinician to plea bargain a man for release who was on death row. He was President of the Southern California Society of

Clinical Hypnosis when they were composed of exclusively MD's, PHD's and DDS'. The year he was president he turned it into a psychoanalytic institute.

Reverse Analysis, the Existential Shift, Gestalt Family Therapy and the Prevention of the Next Holocaust

The purpose of this book is to tell stories that both entertain and bring value to people's lives. The order of the stories told will have no rhyme or reason other than they went through my unconscious mind when I sat down at the typewriter along with the notion they may have value and reach the unconscious minds of the readers in a way that has a better than average chance of entertaining the reader. As I am seventy-five years old when beginning this book, I have worn many hats during my lifetime, and the stories run the gamut.

REVERSE ANALYSIS, THE EXISTENTIAL SHIFT, GESTALT FAMILY THERAPY AND THE PREVENTION OF THE NEXT HOLOCAUST

Dr. Len Bergantino, Ed.D., Ph.D.

The purpose of this book is to open up the space so that the reader – society at large, psychotherapists and patients might start contributing to LIFE FORCE AND THE THERAPEUTIC USE OF SELF IN CREATING A SOCIETY THAT IS UPWARD SPIRALING INSTEAD OF ONE DOMINATED BY INCURABLE DEATH FORCE! FOR THIS TO HAPPEN SOCIETY AT LARGE MUST LEARN TO THINK AND PAY ATTENTION TO THE FACTS IN THIS BOOK THAT WILL PERMIT THE CREATION OF NEW THOUGHT TO MEET NEW PROBLEMS; SO THAT WE DO NOT HAVE SITUATIONS LIKE 127 VETERANS A DAY COMMITTING SUICIDE WITHOUT HOPE THAT THERE ARE ANY TREATMENTS FOR THEM NOW OR THAT CAN BE CREATED! IT IS RECOMMENDED THAT THIS BOOK BE READ AS ONE OF A SERIES OF FOUR WRITTEN BY DR. LEN BERGANTINO TO CREATE THIS NEW SOCIETY! WHILE PSYCHOTHERAPY IS THE MEDIUM OF CHOICE IN TH THIS BOOK, THE FOURTH BOOK UTILIZES MUSIC AS THE MEDIUM TO ANSWER SHAKESPEARE'S QUESTIONS "TO BE OR NOT TO BE!!!!!!!!!!!!!!!!!!!!!!!"

My Children and I were sent back on a karmic mission to PREVENT THE APOCALYPSE AND WE HAVE DONE OUR PART IN WRITING FOUR BOOKS. NOW IT IS UP TO YOU TO READ AND UTILIZE THEM! GOD HAS MYSTERIOUSLY MURDERED THREE PERSONS WHO COULD HAVE STOPPED ME FROM FULFILLING THIS MISSION! WE HAVE SUCCEEDED! THE REST IS UP TO YOU OR YOUR ROOMS WILL BE RESERVED IN HELL! Twelve out of 100 million make it into Heaven!

Xlibris

ISBN 978-1-7960-2117-2
51999

"This book is a one-session existential shift in a lifelong personality characteristic of a patient"

The Art of Psychotherapy and the Liberation of the Therapist

This is a book for professional psychotherapists, psychoanalysts and counselors, students in those areas of specialty and laypersons who are interested in the essence of effective therapy and how some of the people who do it best practice their art. For professionals, the book presents a personal way of viewing therapy that can add pleasurable options. Each of the therapists with whom Bergantino worked, and himself, all had a feeling of enjoyment that they hope will carry over to the office and practices of the readers. For students of therapy, the book offers a search for a professional stature and working posture that may be of value in the development of each student's unique personal style. For laypersons, the book speaks of therapy that can make an impact and speaks of how some of the most potent therapists practice.

ORDER A COPY NOW!

The Art of Psychotherapy And the Liberation of the Therapist

Much has been written about the Science of Psychotherapy, but it has remained for Dr. Bergantino to write about the Art of Psychotherapy with such elegant impact.

Dr. Len Bergantino, Ed.D., Ph.D.

This is a book for professional psychotherapists, psychoanalysts, and counselors; students in those areas of specialty; and lay persons who are interested in the essence of effective therapy and how some of the people who do it best practice their art. For professionals, the book presents a personal way of viewing therapy that can add pleasurable options. Each of the therapists with whom I worked, and myself, all had a feeling of enjoyment that we hope will carry over to the office and practices of the readers. For students of therapy, the book offers a search for a professional stature and working posture that may be of value in the development of each student's unique personal style. For lay persons, the book speaks of therapy that can make an impact and speaks of how some of the most potent therapists practice. For Psychoanalysts interested in the work of the Great British Psychoanalyst, Dr. Wilfred R. Bion MRCS (Medical Royal College of Surgeons), This is the only book that demonstrates exactly what he did.

I wrote the book with the intention of having it be both an experience and an explanation. I have presented it according to my developmental needs while maturing personally and professionally. This was done so the book might be informative at the conscious level, entertaining at the child level, and persuasive at the unconscious level.

The existential moment is the thread that ties the book together; it is a moment of therapeutic potency. While all moments are existential by definition, there are certain moments that are more powerful in helping patients live happier and healthier lives. Positive results, whether they be from one session or over the long haul, are partially, if not fully, a result of existential moments.

Xlibris

The Essence of Music

This multi-purpose book serves as a natural model for how musicians, as human beings, deal with each other. It provides a baseline for humans in answering Shakespeare's question, "To be or not to be." Furthermore, the book is substantive and full of depth, enough to be used in music schools no matter what musical genre since it focuses on musicality, pure sound, the art of musicality and peace. It can be utilized in the psychotherapeutic arts, and its content is healing in nature.

The Essence of Music will teach you the ingredients required "TURN NOTES INTO MUSIC!"

Dr. Len Bergantino, Ed.D., Ph.D.

Musicality,
Pure Sound,
The Art of Melody
and Inner Peace

The Essence of Music

Music is the international language, but what is music!?!!?

For The Bergantino-Bredice Family Music was the FAMILY BUSINESS!
My father, Dan Bergantino, always told me, (in terms of what kind of music you listen to) "IF YOU PUT SHIT IN, SHIT WILL COME OUT! (WHEN YOU PLAY MUSIC)

My cousin Louis Bredice told me, "When I first started playing Jazz, I played a lot of notes! Then I realized, all I needed were the right ones!"

My cousin Freddie Bredice had the fastest technique on guitar I had ever seen! The first time I met him was on a gig in 1967. His speed was blinding, faster than a speeding bullet! I was leaning against a wooden beam next to him and when he finished I said, "You must be cousin Fred!" He said, "Yeah, I don't play chords! It fucks up your hands! "Freddie was one of Joe Diorio's guitar teachers and Joe said he still has nightmares about Freddie's speed! Joe was known as the best jazz guitar player in the world among guitar players. I got him to play songs again in a cd entitled "FALLING IN LOVE" where I am playing mandolin and Joe is accompanying me on guitar. This cd can be purchased from orchard records.com and amazon.com . On the top picture: LISA BERGANTINO (left), DR. LEN BERGANTINO (middle), and ALEX BERGANTINO (right).

This is a multi-purpose book in that much as a previously published book entitled "ZEN AND THE ART OF MOTORCYCLE MAINTENANCE" had more to do with human growth than motorcycle maintenance; this book is a natural model of how musicians as human beings deal with each other thereby providing a baseline for humans in answering Shakespeare's question, "TO BE OR NOT TO BE!" FURTHER, THIS BOOK IS SUBSTANTIVE AND DEPTHFUL ENOUGH TO BE USED IN MUSIC SCHOOLS, NO MATTER WHAT MUSIC GENRE, IN THAT IT FOCUSES ON MUSICALITY, PURE SOUND, THE ART OF MELODY AND PEACE' AND IT CAN BE UTILIZED IN THE PSYCHOTHERAPEUTIC ARTS AND ITS CONTENTS ARE HEALING IN NATURE!

THE REVEREND DR. LEN BERGANTINO
PROFESSIONAL MUSICIAN FROM 1996-2012
(AGE 56-76) MUSICIAN'S LOCAL 47
AMERICAN FEDERATION OF MUSICIAN'S

Xlibris

On the bottom picture:
HARRY JAMES - 1942

ISBN 978-1-7960-2916-1
51999
9 781796 029161

When Baseball was King The New York Yankees were King of Baseball

Dr. Len Bergantino's most intense love affair with baseball was between the years 1951 – 1961. Then he went to college and his attentions went elsewhere. Yet, he returned to baseball by reading baseball books on overseas flights and noticed that every time he read about baseball, it brought peace and tranquility to his life. This prompted him to pen **When Baseball was King The New York Yankees were King of Baseball**.

*THE MINIMUM CONDITIONS REQUIRED TO ACHIEVE THE COMPLETE DEVELOPMENT OF YOUR OWN BEING REQUIRES THAT YOU READ EACH OF THE BOOKS IN A MANNER WHERE THE WORK IS INTEGRATED AT A DEEP AND SUBSTANTIVE LEVEL. THE BASEBALL BOOK ROUNDS OUT THE CHILDHOOD FUN ASPECTS OF YOUR PERSONAL DEVELOPMENT.

When Baseball was King
The New York Yankees were
King of Baseball

Dr. Len Bergantino, Ed.D., Ph.D.

This photo was given to me by the Mick himself. (Courtesy of Mickey Mantle)

The Reverend Dr. Len Bergantino is a multi-faceted individual who achieved international prominence in the areas of psychoanalysis, psychotherapy, clinical psychology, and music. His other fields include education and religion, with a precursory knowledge of medicine and law. He is a weathervane in terms of knowing the right thing to do and has the temperament of Che Guevarra in getting it done!

When the Reverend Dr. Len Bergantino grew up, the first thing he had in mind was to wear number 22 and take over for Allie Reynolds, the Super Chief, as the Mainstay of the Mound Staff of the NEW YORK YANKEES!!! The New York Yankees won 5-world series in a row. (1949-1953) !!!

Xlibris

ISBN 978-1-7960-7891-6
51599
9 781796 078916

This photo was given to me by Mick himself. (Courtesy of Mickey Mantle)

Germans – Jews – Holocausts and the Collective Unconscious

This book is comprised of methods and stories that are intended to evoke a one session existential shift in the reader's grasp of the entire situation in a way that supplants the word "appropriate" with the words "finer and finer discriminations of pure being" and the addition of the words "creative aggression" as an authentic working tool!

Sincerely,

Dr. Len Bergantino, Ed.D., Ph.D.

Author Dr. Len Bergantino, Ed.D., writes letters that are addressed to editors, professors and some of the known political figures such as Senator Bernie Sanders, Congresswoman Tulsi Gabbard, Senator Sheila Keuhl, Chancellor Angela Merkel of Germany, Queen Elizabeth, President Donald Trump. He expresses his stands on some issues using psychological perspective in an honest and conversational way as possible.

Excerpt taken from the conclusion section of the book:

This book has nothing to do with the politics of the word "appropriate" and how those that read it may try to spin it. This book has everything to do with the primitive nature of man and what is actually required to educate peoples of all countries from all walks of life, no matter what caste system they knowingly or unknowingly are stuck in! Along the way to my training family therapists at the international level, Dr. Carl Whitaker, M.D., my teacher and mentor from 1979- 1994, in his last verbal communication to me said, "the work is easy! It's the justification that is hard!" So I will merely present you the facts as they occurred. I will provide no justification for any of it, other than to tell you that is what really occurred in an American system of education between 1949 and 1996 and much of it was unexpected and rather shocking to me.

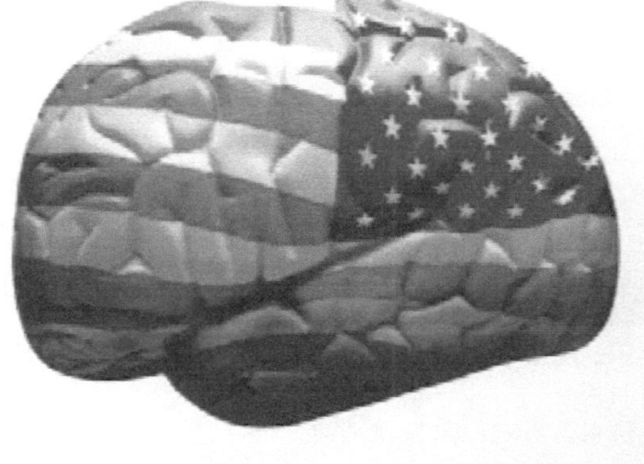

POLITICAL PSYCHOLOGY
INVASIONS

DR. LEN BERGANTINO, Ed.D., Ph.D.

"POLITICAL PSYCHOLOGY INVASIONS"

This book focuses upon the initial psycho-political assessments of the Democratic candidates who were among the sixteen original characters that threw their "hats in the ring!" so to speak! Further, it shows those interested in the current political climate and all other historical political climates HOW TO DIFFERENTIATE REAL NEWS FROM FAKE NEW THROUGH THE DEVELOPMENT AND UTILIZATION OF HIGHER SENSE PERCEPTION.

THE BOOK FURTHER INVADES SEVERAL POLITICAL AND RELIGIOUS TERRITORIES N DEMONSTRATING "HOW TO ASSESS AND DO THE RIGHT THING" AS A WAY OF LIFE, THEREBY AS CITIZENS HELPING TO CREATE AN UPWARD AS OPPOSED TO A DOWNWARD SPIRALING SOCIETY.

IN ADDITION TO ASSESSING AND MAKING DIRECT RECOMMENDATIONS TO THE POPE, AS WELL AS POLITICIANS DIRECT RECOMMENDATIONS ARE MADE SUCH AS THE DOING AWAY WITH LICENSING BOARDS IN THE FIELDS OF PSYCHOANALYSIS, CLINICAL PSYCHOLOGY, PSYCHOTHERAPY, MARITAL AND FAMILY THERAPY AND CLINICAL SOCIAL WORK SO AS NOT TO PROVIDE:

THE GENERAL PUBLIC A FALSE SENSE OF SECURITY WHILE ACTUALLY DESTROYING CLINICIANS" ABILITY TO DO THE WORK THAT CAN ONLY COME WITH THE EVER GROWING THERAPEUTIC USE OF SELF -OR AS SHAKESPEARE UT IT, "TO BE OR NOT TO BE!"

Submitted by Dr. Len   Bergantino, Ed.D., Ph.D.

The Sanctimonious Psychoproctological Invasions: The Handbook for Political Analysis

From 2012 through 2018, Len Bergantino began each day with pro bono writings and invasive interventions that insist and expand upon the first amendment rights of United States citizens. In all areas, he is both knowledgeable and feels national, state, and local governments are stuck in socially immobile positions. He created ways to invade entire cultures and governments to move those stuck in quicksand off the dime and into a society that spirals upward. He refers to the creation of these methods as sanctimonious psychoproctological invasions in the creation of a political psychology that should be studies by all human beings who want to make a difference and give meaning to their lives.

Publisher: Dorrance Publishing Co

To Order a copy of The Sanctimonious Psychoproctological Invasions (ISBN 978-1-6461-0238-9)

Email: bookorders@rosedogbooks.com

Or call 1-800-788-7654 (Mon-Fri) 9AM-4PM

The Denial of Reverse Racism in America

Do you think that some slug who looks very professional who "whispers" an occasional interpretation to you five times a week for 7 years can make one bit of difference in your life or does such a psychotoxic slug called a psychoanalyst merely stick you in an emotional toilet bowl for seven years having the cumulative result of turning you into a hopeless bastard who will never turn the tragic corner in his or her life?
Can your analyst analyze an archaic liquid symbiotic or an osmotic transference, or can they even recognize this phenomena in order to analyze it? If the psychoanalyst cannot analyze these transferences they can't do an analysis!

I used to get "good faith" patients who had the balls to work on the cutting edge at the same time I did because they had had combinations of twenty years of two seven year analyses plus several briefer psychotheraphies, only to be as crazy as the day they walked in! (-$200,000.00)

As Dr. Donald Rinsley, M.D., fellow-American College of Psychoanalysts wrote about me, my work has both a healing effect and affect. Patients used to pay me six months in advance to hold the time open because I was irreplaceable; I was the only one who could analyze the psychotic core of the personality and I was the only who could actually do what Dr. Wilfred R. Bion, MRCS (Medical Royal College of Surgeons) wrote about analyzing the psychotic core of the personality/

As I am seventy-six years old, I have written five books that must be read and digested in their entirety. As these books are the thing-in-itself they will transform the reader into the kinds of analyst, patient and psychotherapist who can make a difference in helping people turn the tragic corner in their lives! In other words, these five books are analysis!

These books were written to be around for a few hundred years and were directly guided by the Almighty!

PRESS RELEASE FOR "THE DENIAL OF REVERSE RACISM IN AMERICA"

THIS BOOK IS INTENDED TO HELP BLACK PEOPLE – PARTICULARLY THOSE IN ADMINISTRATIVE POSITIONS AT THE TOP FOR TREATING WHITE PEOPLE AT THE BOTTOM OF THE TOTEM POLE WHILE DOING IN THE BEST AND BRIGHTEST OF THEIR OWN BLACK CHILDREN AND FALSELY BLAMING IT ON WHITES so as to provide a psychotic PROTECTION GAME OF BLACKS THAT BOTH DO IN THEIR OWN YOUTH AND NEVER ROLL OVER ON ANY BLACK BROTHER OR SISTER THAT REMINDS THEM OF TWO HUNDRED YEARS OF SLAVERY WHILE AT THE SAME TIME PRETENDING TO BE FAIR BY USING "GUILT" AS A MANIPULATION TO JUSTIFY KEEPING "WHITE BOY" AT THE BOTTOM OF THE SOLUTION IS SIMPLE BUT NOT EASY! "BLACK BOY" THE TOTEM POLE! HAS TO STOP BLAMING AND LAYING "GUILT TRIPS" ON MODERNS "WHITE BOY" FOR HIS FOREFATHERS' SINS!"

THIS NEEDS IMMEDIATE CORRECTION IF "WHITE BOY" IS NOT TO BUILD SUCH PRIMITIVE RESENTMENT AT THE UNCONSCIOUS LEVEL THAT YOU GET ONE NEWSLINE AFTER THE OTHER THAT "WHITE BOY" COP SHOOTS BLACK TWELVE YEAR OLD KID RUNNING AWAY IN THE BACK! THIS BOOK PROVIDES AN INTERIM STEP FOR BOTH BLACKS AND WHITES TO EXAMINE THEIR OWN UNDERLYING RACIAL THOUGHTS AND FEELINGS IN A MANNER THAT BRINGS THE SUBCONSCIOUS AND UNCONSCIOUS MORE TO THE SURFACE IN A WAY THAT HELPS THOSE WHO SO ENDEAVOR TO FIND ONGOING SOLUTIONS TO DEAL WITH THE PRIMITIVE REMNANTS OF CRIMES COMMITTED THROUGH TWO HUNDRED YEARS OF SLAVERY! FOR EXAMPLE, I WAS GETTING DONE IN BY A WAITER IN KOLN, GERMANY OF ITALIAN DESCENT in 1990 IN AN ITALIAN RESTAURANT AND THE OWNER SAID HE HATED AMERICANS BECAUSE GENERAL PATTON KILLED HIS ENTIRE FAMILY WHEN COMING THROUGH ITALY IN 1944!

PRESS RELEASE FOR "THE GREATEST BASKETBALL PLAYER I EVER SAW"

To notice greatness and not deny greatness in others you have to notice details that ordinary people often claim do not exist. As ordinary people would much rather blame the victim rather than do their own personal work of self-development. They often deny greatness in others to protect themselves from looking at their own shortcomings often through "hatred and deceptive manipulation (malevolent omnipotence!) Such was the case with Billy Finn, who were he not surrounded by assholes would have averaged fifty two points a game instead of merely holding the state record of fifty two points in one game!

Greatness Kobe Bryant, Elgin Baylor, Larry Bird, Magic Johnson, Bill Russell, LeBron James are all great and have an element of greatness that I have never seen surpassed in my 77 years. Kobe Bryant and LeBron James came into the national basketball association or NBA as it is called right out of high school.

***When Billy Finn played there was no such option! Bob Cousy, famed guard told him he had nothing to teach him in the seventh grade!

***Billy Finn was to basketball what Willie mays was to baseball – the most exciting ballplayer that ever lived despite elements of greatness in others. For example, Ted Williams was the greatest hitter I ever saw. I saw him take batting practice. He hit consecutive line drives so hard they nearly bounced back to 2nd base. This book lays out the details of what made Billy Finn the greatest basketball player who ever lived!

PRESS RELEASE
FOR
"THE GREATEST BASKETBALL PLAYER I EVER SAW"

TO NOTICE GREATNESS AND NOT DENY GREATNESS IN OTHERS YOU HAVE TO NOTICE DETAILS THAT ORDINARY PEOPLE OFTEN LEARNED NOT TO SEE, AS ORDINARY PEOPLE WOULD MUCH RATHER BLAME THE VICTIM RATHER THAN DO THEIR OWN PERSONAL WORK OF SELF DEVELOPMENT. THEY OFTEN DENY GREATNESS IN OTHERS TO PROTECT THEMSELVES FROM LOOKING AT THEIR OWN SHORTCOMINGS OFTEN THROUGH "HATRED AND DECEPTIVE MANIPULATION (MALEVOLENT OMNIPOTENCE)" SUCH WAS THE CASE WITH BILLY FINN, WHO WERE HE NOT SURROUNDED BY ASSHOLES WOULD HAVE AVERAGED FIFTY TWO POINTS A GAME INSTEAD OF MERELY HOLDING THE STATE RECORD OF FIFTY TWO POINTS IN ONE GAME.

GREATNESS KOBE BRYANT, ELGIN BAYLOR, LARRY BIRD, MAGIC JOHNSON, BILL RUSSELL, LEBRON JAMES ARE ALL GREAT AND HAVE AN ELEMENT OF GREATNESS THAT I HAVE NEVER SEEN SURPASSED IN MY 71 YEARS. KOBE BRYANT AND LEBRON JAMES CAME INTO THE NATIONAL BASKETBALL ASSOCIATION (NBA) AS IT IS CALLED RIGHT OUT OF HIGH SCHOOL.

WHEN BILLY FINN PLAYED THERE WAS NO SUCH OPTION? BOB COUSY CAME OUT AND TOLD HIM HE HAD NOTHING TO TEACH HIM IN THE SEVENTH GRADE.

BILLY FINN WAS TO BASKETBALL WHAT WILLIE MAYS WAS TO BASEBALL, THE MOST EXCITING BALLPLAYER THAT EVER LIVED DESPITE ELEMENTS OF GREATNESS IN OTHERS. FOR EXAMPLE, TED WILLIAMS WAS THE GREATEST HITTER I EVER SAW. I SAW HIM TAKE BATTING PRACTICE, HE HIT CONSECUTIVE LINE DRIVES SO HARD THEY NEARLY BOUNCED BACK TO 2ND BASE. THIS BOOK EXPLAINS THE KIND OF USED THAT WOULD MAKE BILLY FINN THE GREATEST BASKETBALL PLAYER WHO EVER LIVED.

Xlibris

SANCTIMONIOUS PSYCHOPROCTOLOGICAL INVASIONIST

MY LAST SUPERVISOR, DR. BRUNO BETTELHEIM, WAS TRAINED IN FREUD'S ORIGINAL TRAINING GROUP. FREUD TOLD HIM THAT "WILHELM REICH, M.D. WAS FREUD'S MOST GIFTED TRAINING ANALYST."

DR. WILHELM REICH SAID, "IF YOU CAN'T DO POLITICS, YOU CAN'T DO ANALYSIS!" DR. BERGANTINO SAYS, "THAT IS THE KIND OF ANALYSIS THAT REACHES AND TRANSFORMS THE UNDERLYING PSYCHOTIC THINKING DISORDERS, PRIMITIVE MENTAL STATES AND PSYCHOTIC CORE OF THE PERSONALITIES OF WHAT ARE THOUGHT TO BE YOUR EVERYDAY NARCISSISTIC, BORDERLINE AND OBSESSIVE COMPULSIVE PERSONALITY DISORDERS!!

LEN BERGANTINO, Ed.D., Ph.D., A.B.P.P.

Psychoanalysis
(310) 207-9397

p. 2

Clinical Psychologist

A.B.P.P. - Diplomate in Family Psychology
American Board of Professional Psychology

REVIEWS

"When thinking of all the therapist I have ever trained or
seen (including Fritz Perls, M.D., Ph.D.) Bergantino! Him
I think about! Him I consider! He is a man of depth! He is
a man of substance!"

Dr. Donald Rinsley, M.D., (particularly helpful for the Art
of Psychotherapy and the Liberation of the Therapist) wrote,
"A unique feature of Dr. Bergantino's presentation -offering,
FASCINATING AND INSTRUCTIVE INSIGHTS INTO THE THERAPUTIC LABORS
OF ADMITTEDLY GIFTED THERAPISTS."

Dr. Carl Whitaker, M.D. wrote "The approach to his own craziness,
the freedom from the culture bind, and the discipline of self
each emerged as obtainable goals of that professional parent we
call the psychotherapist."

Psychiatrist Barry Blichafski wrote "I am happy to recommend
Len Bergantino as an excellent workshop leader, trainer and
psychotherapist...We will be inviting Len Bergantino to return
to AUSTRALIA AND I RECOMMEND HIS WORK, BOTH CLINICAL AND
TEACHING, IN ANY SITUATION.

Betty Erickson, wife of Milton Erickson, M.D. dictated,
"The mutual respect that Dr. Erickson and Dr. Bergantino held
for each other was reflected in the friendship that continued until
Dr. Erickson's death...., and has continued with Dr. Erickson's
widow, Elizabeth Erickson, now 92 years old."

Taro Starak, Gestalt Therapy trainer and Director of International
Gestalt Therapy Training Institute in Brisbane , Australia
said of Dr. Bergantino and the workshops he gave in Australia,
"Dr. Bergantino has a mental precision that electrified the
Australian therapeutic community and had lasting therapeutic
impact."

Clinical Psychologist whose name I cannot locate; "DR. BERGANTINO
IS THE MOST GIFTED CLINICIAN OF HIS TIME!"

MY OWN REVIEW

THE MOST GIFTED CLINICIAN OF ALLTIME! THE BEST THAT EVER LIVED!
IN ADDITION TO WHAT THE MORTALS HAVE SAID ABOUT ME I HAVE
FULFILLED MY KARMIC MISSION AS AGREED UPON AT THE BEGINNING OF
MY CAREER OVER A FIFTY TWO YEAR PERIOD OF TIME AND AS
CONTINUALLY INTERVENDED UPON BY THE HOLY SPIRIT TO ACCOMPLISH
THE TASK ONLY EXPANDED UPON TO INFINITY AS STATED BY
Dr. Robert Dorn, M.D. , Training and Supervising Analyst, who state

1215 Brockton Ave., Ste. 104, W. Los Angeles, CA 90025 - U.S.A.

LEN BERGANTINO, Ed.D., Ph.D., A.B.P.P.

Psychoanalysis
(310) 207-9397

p. 3

Clinical Psychologist

A.B.P.P. - Diplomate in Family Psychology
American Board of Professional Psychology

REVIEWS

Dr. Wilfred R. Bion, MRCS (Medical Royal College of Surgeons,)
the great British psychoanalyst wrote to Dr. Bergantino.
"Your work is evocative and stimulating."

Dr. Milton H. Erickson, M.D. -the Father of Modern Medical
Hypnosis told Dr. Bergantino "I am just an old man who tells
stories. It's your unconscious mind that has the pinpoint
accuracy." "I respect your dedication to the work." And so
Reverse Analysis was born along with a working knowledge of
The Existential Shift.

Dr. Donald Rinsley, M.D., Fellow of The American College of
Psychoanalysts wrote of Dr. Bergantino and his work "There is
no doubt that some people possess a healing capacity and that
others do not"; "I knew at once of your outsiderism...as well
as your talent."

Dr. Carl Whitaker, M.D. - the foremost family therapist at the
international level wrote of Dr. Bergantino, and his work, "He
is a professional reporter of international change models in the
family therapy set and even intrapsychic change process."
Reading his work "is an active experience in the use of self
in the field of psychotherapy, and as such, it both expands
and enriches the community standards of practice of professional
psychotherapists."

Dr. James Grotstein, M.D., Training and Supervising Analyst
wrote of me, "I finally had the pleasure of viewing your tape.
I found it very impressive. It helped me to understand better
where you are coming from and to be able to observe first hand
your intuitive way of approaching people. Your technique reminded
me of an elegant sophistication of Gestalt along with Erickson
and Bion."

Dr. Martin Grotjahn, M.D., Training and Supervising Analyst
wrote "Dr. Bergantino is obviously a gifted therapist..Most
cases as reported in the literature describe the patient's
associations and productions while the therapist remains
hidden in the mystery of darkness unrevealed. Dr. B is an exception;
the great advantage of his work is the openess and frankness with
which the author reveals his experiences when treating patients
or when accepting himself as a patient of another therapist."

Dr. James S. Simkin, Ph.D., -Diplomate-American Board of
Professional Psychology said of Dr. Bergantino.

1215 Brockton Ave., Ste. 104, W. Los Angeles, CA 90025 - U.S.A.

LEN BERGANTINO, Ed.D., Ph.D., A.B.P.P.

Psychoanalysis
(310) 207-9397

Clinical Psychologist

A.B.P.P. - Diplomate in Family Psychology
American Board of Professional Psychology

REVIEWS

WHEN I first started to build my private practice in Beverly Hills,
California, "I think psychoanalysts, psychiatrists and clinical
psychologists have a hard time understanding each other It is like
the Tower of Babel. I think you are the one who can write in a way
whereby they can both understand and talk to each other. Dr. Dorn
wasn't in it for the money. He left Beverly Hills to become Dean
of the Dept. of Psychiatry at Eastern VIrginia Medical School.

I have always loved the BRITS! I gave a workshop in Sheffield,
England at Wentworth Castle entitled "THE THERAPEUTIC
WIZARDRY OF DR. LEN BERGANTINO!" and one at the Royal College of
Medicine entitled "THE DEVELOPMENT AND USE OF EXTRA SENSORY
PERCEPTION IN THE PRACTICE OF PSYCHOANALYSIS, PSYCHOTHERAPY AND
CLINICAL HYPNOSIS". I DELIVERED THE GOODS EACH AND EVERY TIME OUT!

Dr. Len Bergantino, Ed.D., Ph.D.

IN OTHER WORDS WHEN GOD USED THE KARMIC WHEEL TO SEND ME BACK
AS THE REINCARNATED SOULS OF SIGMUND FREUD AND JULIUS CAESAR
AND MY CHILDREN LISA, BACK AS THE REINCARNATED SOULS OF DR.
WILFRED R. BION AND CLEOPATRA AND MY SON ALEX AS THE
REINCARNATED SOULS OF DR. MILTON H. ERICKSON AND BRUTUS,
ASSESSING THAT ALL OF THOSE SKILL SETS WERE NECESSARY TO DO
THE JOB, HOW CAN MY OWN EVALUATION OF ME, MY CLINICAL SKILLS,
AND MY WRITINGS OF ALL FOUR BOOKS BE ANYTHING LESS THAN

I AM THE BEST PSYCHOANALYST OF ALL TIME AND IN ACCORD WITH MY
ORIGINAL IDEA (FREUD -THE LAST TIME AROUND), THE SLOW READING
AND INTEGRATION OF ALL FOUR BOOKS WILL EVOKE AN UPWARD
SPIRALING SOCIETY AND PREVENT BOTH THE NEXT HOLOCAUST AND THE
APOCALIPSE AND FREE FROM THE DESTRUCTION OF THE LINKS TO
KNOWLEDGE AT THE HANDS OF ENVIOUS AND HATEFUL HUMAN MORTAL
COLLEAGUES!

IN OTHER WORDS GOD HAS REVIEWED ME AND MY WORK AND ANYONE ELSE
PALES IN COMPARISON!

I Am Freud! Psychoanalysis Is the Only Method of Cure: It's Too Bad No One Knows How to Do One!!!

This book shows how extrasensory perception can be developed, utilized by the therapeutic use of self, and help pinpoint psychophysiological awareness, which can prevent disease and circumvent disease in later life.

www.xlibris.com

ISBN 13 (SOFT): 978-1-9845-5729-2

ISBN 13 (HARD): 978-1-9845-5730-8

ISBN 13 (eBook): 978-1-9845-5728-5

ORDER A COPY NOW!

Reverse Analysis, the Existential Shift, Gestalt Family Therapy and the Prevention of the Next Holocaust

This is a clinical example of a one-session existential shift in a lifelong personality characteristic of a patient. This is for hypnosis or training in hypnosis contact.

www.xlibris.com

ISBN 13 (SOFT): 978-1-7960-2117-2

ISBN 13 (HARD): 978-1-7960-2118-9

ISBN 13 (eBook): 978-1-7960-2116-5

ORDER A COPY NOW!

The Art of Psychotherapy and the Liberation of the Therapist

This is a book for professional psychotherapists, psychoanalysts and counselors, students in those areas of specialty and laypersons who are interested in the essence of effective therapy an how some of the people who do it best practice their art.

www.xlibris.com

ISBN 13 (SOFT): 978-1-7960-2422-7
ISBN 13 (HARD): 978-1-7960-2423-4
ISBN 13 (eBook): 978-1-7960-2421-0

The Essence of Music

This multi-purpose book serves as a natural model for how musicians, as human beings, deal with each other.

www.xlibris.com

ISBN 13 (SOFT): 978-1-7960-2916-1
ISBN 13 (HARD): 978-1-7960-2917-8
ISBN 13 (eBook): 978-1-7960-2915-4

When Baseball was King The New York Yankees were King of Baseball

Come and join Dr. Len Bergantino as he recounts and celebrates the glory of The New York Yankees.

www.xlibris.com

ISBN 13 (SOFT): 978-1-7960-7891-6

ISBN 13 (eBook): 978-1-7960-8028-5

ORDER A COPY NOW!

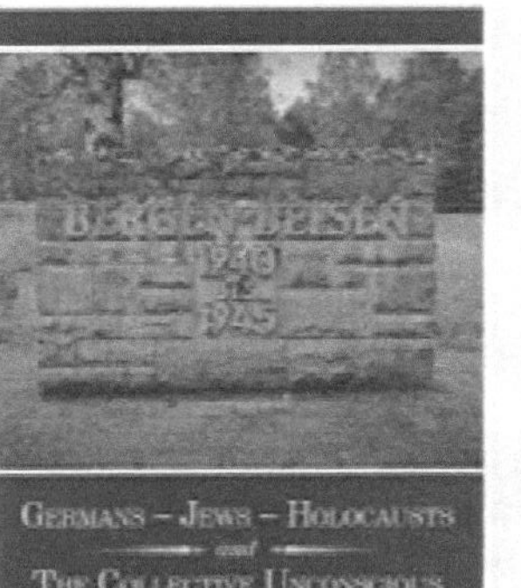

Germans – Jews – Holocausts and the Collective Unconscious

There is no available information at this time. Author will provide once available.

www.xlibris.com

ISBN 13 (SOFT): 978-1-7960-8445-0

ISBN 13 (eBook): 978-1-7960-8446-7

ORDER A COPY NOW!

Political Psychology Invasions

See how Dr. Len Bergantino, Ed.D., Ph.D. assess the Democratic candidates in POLITICAL PSYCHOLOGY INVASIONS.

www.xlibris.com

ISBN 13 (SOFT): 978-1-7960-2916-1
ISBN 13 (HARD): 978-1-7960-2917-8
ISBN 13 (eBook): 978-1-7960-2915-4

ORDER A COPY NOW!

The Sanctimonious Psychoproctological Invasions: The Handbook for Political Analysis

From 2012 through 2018, Len Bergantino began each day with pro bono writings and invasive interventions that insist and expand upon the first amendment rights of United States citizens. In all areas, he is both knowledgeable and feels national, state, and local governments are stuck in socially immobile positions. He created ways to invade entire cultures and governments to move those stuck in quicksand off the dime and into a society that spirals upward. He refers to the creation of these methods as sanctimonious psychoproctological invasions in the creation of a political psychology that should be studies by all human beings who want to make a difference and give meaning to their lives.

ORDER A COPY NOW!

Publisher: Dorrance Publishing Co

To Order a copy of The Sanctimonious Psychoproctological Invasions (ISBN 978-1-6461-0238-9)
Email: bookorders@rosedogbooks.com
Or call 1-800-788-7654 (Mon-Fri) 9AM-4PM

www.ingramcontent.com/pod-product-compliance
Lightning Source LLC
Chambersburg PA
CBHW022115050726
47591CB00002B/799